Morarji Desai

Morarji Desai
A Profile in Courage

Arvindar Singh

Foreword by
Sir Mark Tully

PAPER MISSILE
NIYOGI BOOKS

Published by
NIYOGI BOOKS
Block D, Building No. 77,
Okhla Industrial Area, Phase-I,
New Delhi-110 020, INDIA
Tel: 91-11-26816301, 26818960
Email: niyogibooks@gmail.com
Website: www.niyogibooksindia.com

Editor: Gita Rajan
Design: Nabanita Das

ISBN: 978-93-89136-01-2
Publication: 2019

Printed at: Niyogi Offset Pvt. Ltd., New Delhi, India

Contents

Contents

Foreword

I see Morarji Desai or Morarji as I will call him from here onwards, as one of the most important figures in modern Indian history, particularly the history of India after Independence. Just look at his record as set out in Arvindar Singh's biography – Chief Minister of one of the largest states, Finance Minister in the Central Government, twice an unsuccessful candidate to be Prime Minister, Deputy Prime Minister, one of the top leaders of the movement which led Indira Gandhi to impose the Emergency, and when she was defeated Morarji at last became Prime Minister. He was the first Prime Minister of India who was not a member of the Congress party.

Morarji was a remarkable person too. He modelled his life on the principles of Mahatma Gandhi and continued his practice of spinning to the end of his life. Even as Prime Minister he always wore immaculate white khadi. I remember watching him as Prime Minister telling autograph seekers that he would only sign for those who promised to wear khadi for the rest of their lives. His Gandhian respect for truth underpinned his political career. This led him into confrontations with superiors when he was a civil servant of the British Raj government and with his colleagues throughout his long political career. Inevitably he acquired a reputation for being stubborn whereas strict would be a better word. His strictness meant he was not always easy to live with. Although an obvious candidate to be Prime Minister when Nehru died, his colleagues ganged up to prevent that, as they did when Shastri died. His habit, which he wrote about, of drinking a small quantity of his urine every day, made him appear eccentric to many. Prohibition is not popular with elite and with Morarji it was almost an obsession. As a result of his fierce independent-mindedness, his swimming against the stream, Morarji has tended to be written off as an oddball, or perhaps I should say maverick, rather than a man who played a unique role in Indian politics, and a man to be admired for his principled life.

India's history would certainly have been different if Morarji had been chosen to be Prime Minister in 1964. Dynastic politics would not have developed, no undermining democracy within the Congress party, the autonomy of the institutions of India would have been respected, the rule of law upheld. His record makes this clear.

Morarji's period as Prime Minister was ended prematurely by the irresponsibility of politicians who, although they had experienced the collapse of democracy during the emergency, allowed themselves to be driven by self-interest rather than the urgent need to re-establish a stable, principled, government. Instead of cooperating with each other to meet that need they tore their own government down and left the way open for Indira Gandhi to return. In this way they deprived India of the only opportunity it has had to establish a stable two-party system.

The downfall of the Morarji-led Janata government has meant that its achievements have been forgotten. Much of the credit for those achievements must go to Morarji. Arvindar has listed them. I would like to mention a few which indicate how different Indian history might have been if Morarji's government had lasted longer.

The first and most obvious achievement was the re-establishment of the rule of law and passing legislation intended to prevent lawlessness ever returning. Morarji not only gave freedom back to the fourth pillar upholding the rule of law, the press, he encouraged journalists to question him and his government at regular press conferences, in sharp contrast to India's last two Prime Ministers. Furthermore he set up a committee to suggest ways of freeing the electronic media from the chains of officialdom, so the Morarji government could have led to the establishment of genuine independent public service broadcasting which would have had a profound impact on the development of the electronic media. He held the first ever genuinely free election in Kashmir and was discussing the Kashmir issue with General Zia of Pakistan. Even if it is sheer folly to imagine those talks could have led to a settlement of the Kashmir issue, one can suggest that beautiful, tragic, state would be a very different place today if Indira Gandhi hadn't undermined the trust between the people of Kashmir and the government resulting from Morarji's election by dismissing the Chief Minister Farooq Abdullah. Rajiv Gandhi then gave Pakistan the opportunity to intervene in Kashmir by rigging the subsequent election.

Arvindar's biography reminds us today that such an upright principled politician as Morarji can and indeed did exist in India. It leaves me with a deep sense of sadness that today there is no leading politician with such a profound respect for the rule of law, and indeed the other laws of democracy. There is sadness too in being reminded of the tragic wasted opportunity the collapse of the Janata Government represents. It says something about India today that a truly admirable Indian, someone worthy of emulation, is forgotten today. Let's hope Arvindar's biography will revive the memory of Morarji. It's written by an admirer and a friend of Morarji, but it's not just a hagiography, ignoring the mistakes he made, his faults, and his angularity; it's a worthy tribute to a man I, like Arvindar, greatly admire.

Mark Tully
London
January 2019

Preface

Morarji Desai was Prime Minister of India for two-and-a-half years (24 March 1977 to 28 July 1979) which can by no stretch of imagination be called a long period in the history of the Indian Republic or for that matter any country that practises a democratic form of governance. But the circumstances in which he assumed office and the achievements of his government in that relatively short period were, in many ways, to make a permanent impact on the body politic of India, which is, till today, looked back upon with gratitude by many of his countrymen, particularly those who have lived through those fateful years.

What was the situation when he took over as the head of the first Non-Congress government to rule India? An Emergency of 19 months, a constitutional dictatorship with the press muzzled with absolute censorship, a total of 1,50,000 people languishing in jail without trial, civil liberties suspended and a rule of tyranny and fear prevailing throughout the country would briefly describe the situation in India before the 1977 elections to parliament.

After his first press conference as Prime Minister (which also incidentally was his first engagement as Prime Minister), he religiously stuck to the schedule of a monthly press conference throughout the 27 months he held office. In that conference, he outlined the basic priorities of his government and during the interaction with the media, he highlighted, as his basic goals, the austerity proposed to be practised in government, complete freedom of the press, implementation of socialist policies as this meant equality in all spheres and amending the Constitution as to remove the draconian provisions which had been added during the Emergency. It can be said that during the short period the Janata Party was in power the government strived towards achievements in all the areas mentioned.

On taking over the Prime Ministership it is also worth mentioning that he paid tribute to India's first Prime Minister Jawaharlal Nehru in one of his early interviews and described him as 'a democrat in his bones and blood and marrow' (*Time* Magazine, 4 April 1977). This was despite the fact that his government had many parties as its constituents opposed to Congress policies since Independence.

He enjoyed the cut and thrust of debate both inside Parliament and outside. During his encounter with the fourth estate immediately on assumption of the post of Prime Minister, he said, 'Ask any question, I will not take it ill, but you should also not take it ill when I say something not very pleasant or palatable.' He was not one to show intolerance to an interviewer no matter how harsh the tone of the scribe interviewing him.

This book deals with Morarji in the various phases of his life. He has been called a Gandhian and probably was one of the last of that breed. Most of his ministerial posts were held in Congress administrations except, of course, the Prime Ministership, which was an outcome of the unusual circumstances of the Janata Party victory in 1977.

Born in the small hamlet of Bhadeli in Bulsar District of Gujarat he covered the long and arduous journey to the Prime Minister's residence in New Delhi.

Morarji, the administrator par excellence, has been adequately covered in the volume; this is justifiably so as right from his days in what was then the undivided Bombay Province, his administrative skills were held in high esteem by both politicos and bureaucrats alike. As his Press Adviser H.Y. Sharda Prasad has written, 'He was a first rate administrator; one of the best in free India. He could seize a problem or a file by its head and its tail. He asked the right questions and came to the right conclusions. He had too much common sense and knowledge of the rules and precedents to be fooled by the bureaucracy ... No future Prime Minister will think, as he did, that the people have to be "improved" morally. They will rather play up to the people.'

Morarji was undoubtedly a man of principle who had the image of being remote and forbidding, which his biographers D.F. Karaka and G.S. Bhargava have noted in their works on him and which is also the popular impression of the man. However, once one got to know him the story was a different one, which I have made note of in this book. The real man was warm and had a good sense of humour. I may add that both these distinguished biographers have also given evidence of these traits of his personality in their respective books on Morarji.

I met Morarji Desai when he was in retirement, after his active political career had come to an end. In the 13 years that he lived after our first meeting we met on numerous occasions in Delhi and Mumbai. Since he lived in Mumbai then, most of the meetings were confined to that city. To meet him was not at all complicated as it is with many pompous political leaders one comes across nowadays; one walked into his house and had a word with Chandra Kant Tawade who looked after his appointments and one was with him in a few minutes; the only time one had to wait was if he already had a visitor with him. This, as I came to know, was the way of the old guard, the leaders who had won independence for the nation and believed they had to be in touch with the people as much as was humanly feasible.

Morarji Desai was also extremely prompt in answering letters and mostly used the postcard. Below is the text of a post card written to me on 28 September 1983 (The facsimile of the original postcard can be seen in the photo section of the book).

Dear Shri Arvindar Singh,

I was glad to receive your letter of 24th today.

I am very happy that you are following the same principles of life which I believe in and do my best to follow. This will give you complete peace of mind. In doing this one has to be fearless, truthful, non-violent in thought word and deed, and humble; if any of these four weakens, all weaken.

If you do your best to follow them God will guide you and no human guidance will be necessary.

I shall be passing through Delhi on the 1st evening and 3rd morning. I shall be at 29, Jorbagh from 7:30 to 9:00 pm on the 1st and from 7:00 to 8:30 am on the 3rd.

Yours sincerely,
Morarji Desai

Such communication between us took place regularly as he did not believe in the technique of saying 'ask my secretary for an appointment' or 'ring up and then come' a mode followed by many present day big-wigs. In this regard once, on being asked what was the most interesting aspect of his life, Morarji had answered, 'The fact that I have been able to serve the people. Even today, whether I am ill or well, I am always accessible to anyone who wants to meet me. That has always been my way. I have believed that power is short-lived. One must learn to serve ... After all, my time is not for myself, it is for others.' (Interview with Pritish Nandy, *The Illustrated Weekly of India*, 2 February, 1986).

It was quite often that I saw him during the last years of his life in Mumbai. I attended his last birthday celebration on 28 February 1995, at his residence when he entered his 100th year. My last meeting with him was on 4 March 1995 and he bid me goodbye after the meeting saying, 'I am always happy to see you.' He passed away on 10 April 1995, barely a month and a week later.

This book was earlier written and published in 1994 to coincide with the Morarji Desai Centenary which was to begin in 1995. The present volume has been suitably updated with additional material.

Early Life
(1896-1930)

Morarji Desai was born in Bhadeli, a village in Bulsar district of Gujarat, on 29th February 1896, a leap year. His father, Ranchodji Desai, was a school teacher in the erstwhile Bhavnagar State of Saurashtra, Gujarat. Right from his childhood, Morarji was good at studies. He had to walk three miles to and from school, everyday. In addition to studies, he had to also attend to household chores on a daily basis, tending the cattle being one of them. This was an experience and a chore he thoroughly enjoyed. Morarji was barely fifteen years old when his father met with a tragic end when he fell into a well and died. Though it was an accidental death, rumours floated around that he had committed suicide. The timing of the death was really unfortunate as Morarji's wedding to Gajraben was scheduled for the very next day.

For Morarji, his father remained his guiding spirit throughout his life. From him Morarji imbibed a deep religious faith, a sense of peaceful equanimity and self-respect. A framed picture of his father was always with him. After the death of his father, Morarji had to take on the role of the bread-winner for the family. He was the eldest of six children. He continued to excel in studies and gave tuitions to supplement the family income.

He was an avid reader and had thoroughly mastered the Ramayana, Mahabharata and the Panchtantra. These texts laid the firm foundation for the basic values of truth, morality and spirituality he imbibed and upheld during his entire life. After completing schooling, passing the Matriculation examination in first class in January 1913, Morarji left for Bombay to continue his studies. He completed his degree course from Wilson College, Bombay.

During his college days, Morarji stayed in Goculdas Tejpal Boarding House. The first session of the Indian National Congress was held in 1885 in the compound of this Boarding House. Morarji spent four and a half years in Bombay. During his stay there, he used to play tennis in the afternoons and loved going for long walks. A book titled *Physical Culture Encyclopaedia* which he read during his college days, introduced him to nature cure which he then practised throughout his life. During the Intermediate Course, he suddenly suffered from a feeling of nervousness during the examinations owing to which he could secure a mere pass without any distinction or good marks; the nervousness was probably brought on by the pressure from his maternal uncle who had also insisted on Morarji aiming for and securing a first class at all costs.

However, during his B.Sc. examinations he fared much better. Not being inclined towards frivolous entertainment, during his college days, he had not frequented theatres or cinema halls, nor seen any film or plays except rare occasions when he had to go with friends who insisted on his company. He was more interested in sports and loved to watch tennis tournaments and cricket matches and other sporting events.

This was a period when India and Indians were awakening politically. It was hence but natural that Morarji Desai too attended some sessions of the Indian National Congress. He was the Secretary of his college debating society. In that capacity, he once had an opportunity to invite Mrs Sarojini Naidu to speak in his college. He never forgot the kindness and affection with which she responded to his request. Her wonderful speech and her command over the language enthralled the students.

By the time he left college, Morarji underwent a personality change. From a timid youth, he metamorphosed into a fearless young man with courage, conviction in his beliefs and strength of character. After completing his BSc, in 1917, he was thinking on the lines of pursuing studies further; doing post-graduation and choosing academics as his career, aiming to become a professor. By June-July 1917, Morarji Desai, on the persuasion of his professor, sent in an application for the Provincial Civil Service (Revenue). The University Training Corps (UTC) had been established in various universities due to pressure by nationalist leaders for Indian participation in the Army. Morarji Desai joined the UTC. After about two months training in Bombay, he went to Pune to attend the Corps camp. He was soon appointed a Commissioned Officer. The camp life inculcated in him training and discipline, which stood him in good stead all through his public life. He was given an outstanding certificate at the end of his camp. His Officer-in-Charge said that he would be an asset to the then Provincial Civil Service (PCS). He was called for an interview in March, 1918. During the course of the PCS interview, towards the end, he was asked what would be his reaction if he did not get the job. Morarji's spontaneous reply, brimming with self confidence, was, 'The world is wide and I am young. I am sure to get a good job elsewhere.' Impressed by his confident and fearless response, a special vacancy was created by this Board especially for him.

Morarji Desai could have joined the Indian Civil Service (ICS) or got a King's Commission in the army. But he chose not to pursue either of these courses, as it would have meant going to England for training for two years, leaving behind his family. He felt it would be inhuman and unfair to his family members leaving them to fend for themselves. Therefore, he joined the Provincial Civil Service as a probationary Deputy Collector, in Ahmedabad, in May 1918. At that time a Deputy Collector had to perform both judicial as well as executive functions. Within about six months Morarji Desai had passed the probationary examination and was qualified to be a first class magistrate. Chatfield was the Collector under whom he had to serve his first posting. Morarji used to tour the taluks, towns and villages under his jurisdiction. He gained a fair amount of experience as a magistrate, deciding various types of cases including criminal and other disputes.

In 1920, he was transferred as Deputy Collector, Thane. While at Thane, he was instrumental in streamlining the administration in the Collectorate. All this experience helped him to blossom into one of the finest administrators of modern India. During this tenure, he came to know that a *shirastedar* working under him was a man of dubious character given to taking advantage of his position and resorting to illegal acts. Morarji's boss, the Collector, had warned him about this when

Morarji took charge. Within a month Morarji found something amiss in one of the files sent to him. The file, hidden amongst the regular pile of files sent to him, a routine practice in government offices, did not escape Morarji's eagle eye and sharp scrutiny. It was to do with the transfer of a *talati*. Morarji sent back the file, without concurrence to the proposed course of action, but it promptly re-appeared the next day. Morarji sent it back yet again. It was again presented to him the third day. After this third appearance, he sent for the *shirastedar* and asked him to justify the course of action proposed in the file. The man stood silent, having no reasonable explanation to offer. Morarji warned him not to repeat such dubious acts and ordered him to be honest and straightforward in his dealings. Realising he was working under an upright officer who was sharp and would not tolerate any misdemeanour, the *shirastedar* mended his ways and brought in integrity and efficiency in his work. Within a year Morarji noticed the improvement and recommended his promotion to the next grade. He was accordingly appointed as a *chitnis* in the Collector's office. Though the Collector knew of this man's previous reputation and had warned Morarji about him, still he did not monitor his working in the new post to ensure his dealings were honest and efficient. Seeing the superiors lax and no longer watchful, the fellow, now a *chitnis*, quickly slipped back into his old ways.

When Thane district was reorganised, Morarji was shifted from Thane to Kalyan, the district headquarters. In Thane district the thieves were very cunning. Once when on camp, Morarji fell victim to these notorious thieves. His confidential box, a brass box and a gold watch from his pocket were all stolen. It was done so silently and stealthily that he heard nothing.

On another occasion, the local Deputy Superintendent of Police's (DSP) pistol was stolen. The pistol was under his pillow, and the thief had sat near his head for half an hour, slipping the pistol out slowly; later he was caught. By December 1922, Morarji left Kalyan for Broach, now Bharuch. The people of Kalyan gave him a very warm send off at the time and many people had tears in their eyes. He was posted as a Front Officer in Broach District. This post too required him to perform both judicial and executive functions. In Broach, he had to deal with many a criminal case. He observed a rule: not to delay judgement in such cases beyond six weeks to two months. He further made it a rule that the judgement was delivered within six to eight weeks no matter how complicated the case. This earned for him the highest regard and respect of the common people.

Morarji was always forthright in dealing with his seniors, never bothering about the consequences. This was because he had always felt that the straight and truthful path is always the ideal one, it is one which makes one totally fearless. During Morarji Desai's tenure at Broach, one Ziauddin Ahmed was posted as the DSP Broach. As per the practice of sycophancy in vogue during those times, usually the Front Officer would call on any new incumbent posted as DSP. Morarji did not see any reason to observe this unwritten law. When they chanced to meet at a marriage party, the new DSP asked Morarji Desai as to why he had not called on him. Morarji's quick repartee was that since the DSP was the newcomer, he should have called on Morarji

Desai first. A few days later, when there was a farewell for the Collector at the local Gymkhana, the DSP made a comment that the powers and the arms of the police were long and strong. Sensing the comment was for him, Morarji immediately retorted: the powers of a Sub-Divisional Magistrate were much more than that of a police officer. While a police officer could detain a man in custody only for 24 hours, and would need the permission of a magistrate for any detention beyond that period, a Sub-Divisional Magistrate could sentence rigorous imprisonment for any offender for a period up to two years.

Irritated, Ahmed went on so far as to say, 'Young man, you will cool down in course of time.' Morarji was blunt to the point of rudeness. He retorted, 'There would be no need for me to cool down as my family is not used to an expensive life. I can manage to maintain my family on a mere ₹50/- a month, and will always earn much more than that.' The officer soon realised that Morarji had meant him no ill-will. He was blunt and straightforward by nature and not given to sycophancy. He further noticed during their later interactions that Morarji was honest and was quite courteous to him. Hence, over a period of time, they became friends. When Morarji left Broach, Ahmed came to the farewell at the Broach Club, even though he was not a member, and gave a farewell speech in Morarji's honour.

The 1920s was a period of momentous events on the national scene, the Non-Co-operation movement having taken place, with Mahatma Gandhi becoming a national hero. It was the time when the independence struggle became a full-fledged movement and affected most right-thinking patriotic Indians.

At the end of 1924, Morarji was posted as Personal Assistant to the Collector in Godhra district of Gujarat. This was undoubtedly the turning point in his Service with the British Government.

During his tenure at Godhra, he was able to solve a long outstanding dispute between the local electrical company and the municipality regarding the terms and conditions of contract between the two parties. He could resolve the problem between the parties through the means of free and frank dialogue with both parties.

The police in the district, more particularly a *faujdar* called Shahabuddin, had created terror among the people of the region. Morarji proceeded against Shahabuddin as there was evidence of a rape case against him. As he found the evidence quite true and ample, he issued a warrant of arrest against the *faujdar* and sentenced him to imprisonment. This act brought in a sense of relief among the people of Godhra.

It was while he was at Godhra that a riot took place during 1927-28, when on Ganesh Chaturthi day a procession of Hindus playing religious songs and bhajans, passed by a masjid. The DSP at Godhra was the same Ziauddin Ahmed who had earlier been with Morarji Desai at Broach. As the DSP was accompanying the procession there was no attack on it, but while it was dispersing, the participants were attacked. One participant, Purshottam Shah, was killed and many others injured. Morarji reached the place promptly, but his Collector Mr Hartshone, who was basically dishonest, ordered Morarji to go to the hospital and record the statements of the injured. Morarji felt that there was an ulterior motive behind the order – to ask to record statements when people were injured and thus in a confused state. Morarji duly followed the orders, but at the same time noted down the exact time when he entered the hospital as well as the time he recorded the statements. He also noted the time he reached the Collector's house to give him the statements. One Vamanrao Mukadam, the leader of the procession, spread around a rumour that the DSP had instigated the attack and had acted in a communal manner. As this was untrue, Morarji defended the DSP in his statement before the members of the Bombay Assembly who had visited Godhra to inquire about the riot. The DSP and the Collector tried to put pressure on Morarji to tell them what he had deposed before the Members of the Legislative Assembly but he refused to do so as he had to later appear as a witness in the case. A few days later, in consultation with Morarji, the DSP and the Divisional Forest Officer, the Collector and District Magistrate ordered the arrest of some Hindu leaders who, according to him, were causing harassment to some Muslims living in the villages around Godhra. Since one of the four people arrested had lost his father on that very day, he wanted a remission of about 10-12 days to finish the ceremonies. He arranged for a lawyer and applied for bail, along with the other three. Morarji granted the bail as all four gave the necessary sureties and guarantees that they would not disturb the peace till the case was over. His Collector was quite annoyed at this and told him that the Commissioner was interested in the case and Morarji's action of granting bail was viewed with displeasure. He made it quite clear the he was issuing a threat to Morarji for acting against the government's interests, though the act was a humane one and one of natural decency.

Morarji, being blunt, told the Collector to his face that it was impossible to work under him in such circumstances, and sought a transfer as he felt it would be impossible for him, Morarji, to serve the people or the government honestly under that Collector. That put the Collector in his place.

Since there was no clear-cut evidence against the persons accused in the case mentioned above, Morarji acquitted them after taking time to word and record the judgment meticulously and accurately stating all facts of the case with clear-cut precision.

This whole affair created a gloomy and unhealthy atmosphere all around, as the Collector was bent upon taking a prejudiced view and punishing the innocent. The Collector took recourse to a remark made against Morarji Desai during the earlier riot case and instituted a Departmental Inquiry against him.

All these events naturally exposed the hypocrisy and double standards of the Britishers to Morarji Desai, an honest and upright young man. As it is, he had begun toying with the idea of leaving government service, ever since he came to Godhra. As pointed out earlier, this was a period of great political renaissance. Morarji was an avid reader of Gandhiji's *Young India* and *Navjivan*, and this had a profound effect on him. He had started wearing khadi from 1927.

In 1928 or thereabouts Morarji decided to become a celibate and practise Brahmacharya as he did not believe in artificial methods of birth control. He took the consent of his wife before he took this decision. He was quite frank while discussing the subject and mentioned that it was not some strange or freak thought he was putting into practice. He iterated that the Roman

Catholic Church and Mahatma Gandhi advocated this practice and went on to quote Gandhi as having said that using artificial methods of birth control turned women into prostitutes. Though he himself felt that this was too harsh a comment. Once, when an interviewer asked him whether he had forced it on his wife, Morarji replied that his wife was not someone to give in to pressure and that she was equally stubborn and straightforward. The late D.F. Karaka had interviewed Morarji's wife Gajraben where she confirmed the truth of Morarji's statement.

After all these events, that is the Departmental Inquiry and the rest, Morarji went on leave and spent the first four months of 1929, visiting South India.

In May 1929, Morarji rejoined duty as Personal Assistant to the Collector of Ahmedabad. By now, he was thinking seriously of quitting government service and joining the freedom struggle. However, dedicated and meticulous in the discharge of duties as he was, as soon as he found that his office in Ahmedabad was rather disorganised, he set about reorganising it and making sure that all the arrears were cleared quickly and efficiently. On 12 March 1930, he had an occasion to witness the 'Dandi March' of Mahatma Gandhi. It had a great effect on him and made a deep everlasting impact.

Freedom Fighter and Minister (1930-1952)

On 21 May, 1930, answering the call of destiny, Morarji Desai quit the Provincial Civil Service, which he had served for twelve years. The Departmental Inquiry, which had been initiated on the Godhra incident, had given its report. Morarji was accused of partisan behaviour and brought down four places in the Seniority List of his cadre. The British tended to be biased, more often than not, in their action against Indian officials.

Thus, began a long and chequered public career, the story of which is indeed fascinating. During his first few months in the Congress, he toured a few interior areas of Bombay state, taking active part in the 'no-tax' campaign which was propagated by the Congress among the peasants. He was also in charge of the organisational work in Ahmedabad.

The Congress had been declared 'illegal' by the British in October 1930. Morarji was arrested and kept in Sabarmati Jail at Ahmedabad for his period of imprisonment. While imprisoned thus, he started the practice of having a bath in the morning with cold water stored overnight in earthen pots, even during winter. He also started shaving without soap. His habit of sleeping in the open, summer or winter, helped him develop a good resistance against the cold.

He was released from prison a little earlier than scheduled as a lawyer had challenged the judgment against Morarji on his own account, and it had been declared illegal.

During the Gandhi-Irwin talks of early 1931, during the Civil Disobedience Movement, the Mahatma sent word to Morarji, now very much in the top echelons of the Gujarat Congress, whether he should ask the Viceroy to take him back into government service. Morarji went down to Delhi and told the Mahatma that he had no interest in joining the government as he had left it to work for the freedom of the country. The Mahatma said that he would ask the Viceroy to sanction him a pension. It was duly sanctioned. However, when he was Revenue Minister of Bombay State, Morarji himself voluntarily gave up the right for a pension.

The Gandhi-Irwin pact was signed in March 1931. Shortly thereafter Morarji took over as General Secretary of the Gujarat Congress Committee. During 1932 Morarji courted arrest again and was kept at Sabarmati Jail and then at Nasik Jail. Later he was moved to Yervada Jail.

During his time in prison Morarji invariably carried out experiments. These experiments led him to follow certain principles that later became his trademark – both in his personal life as well as a statesman and politician. While at Nasik Jail, Morarji was a witness to the formation of the Socialist group within the Congress, having Jaya Prakash Narayan, Minoo Masani and Achut Patwardhan as its prominent members.

Some people from this group (mainly Jaya Prakash Narayan) tried to induce Morarji to be a part of it, the bait being that he would have a prominent position, akin to that of Sardar Patel in Gujarat. Morarji, shrewd enough to see through their plans, told them point blank that he would not be a party to such underhand manoeuvres.

Later, when he took over as Congress President at the Lucknow Session in 1935, Jawaharlal Nehru brought back some of these rebelling splinter group members into the mainstream Congress Working Committee. A democrat to the core, Nehru always abided by the majority decisions in the Working Committee.

After his release in 1934, Morarji toured extensively within Gujarat and engrossed himself in the task of building up the Gujarat Congress. He was instrumental in bringing U.N. Dhebar and other such luminaries into the Congress.

In 1935, Morarji visited Sri Aurobindo Ashram at Pondicherry. During his stay at the ashram, he had discussions on spiritual matters with The Mother, Sri Aurobindo's spiritual collaborator who was considered by Sri Aurobindo to be his equal in yogic stature. Since Sri Aurobindo did not engage in personal discussions or interactions, but only replied to queries through letters, Morarji exchanged a letter with Sri Aurobindo.

During this trip, Morarji also visited Ramana Ashram at Tiruvannamalai, the abode of Ramana Maharishi, considered one of the greatest sages from Tamil Nadu and revered by Indians and foreigners alike to this day. When Morarji met him, he was awestruck at the glow emanating from the face of the Maharishi, the glow of a truly evolved and enlightened soul. Morarji felt that

decision. Morarji reiterated that it was not possible. Soon after, Brabourne gave his assent. Lord Brabourne passed away a few months after this meeting. In him, Morarji felt, India lost a true friend. Had he lived and been Viceroy for a full term India could have got freedom much earlier.

When Morarji took over his department, Sir Gilbert Wiles, who was the then Chief Secretary, while paying Morarji a courtesy call, walked into his office, his pipe in his hand. Morarji gave him such an extremely cold look, that flustered, Sir Gilbert promptly put his burning pipe into his coat pocket. Morarji asked him whether he was in the habit of calling on the Governor too pipe in hand. Sir Gilbert immediately realised his behaviour was wrong and uncouth and made amends. As a consequence a good relationship, with the mainstays of decency, courtesy and mutual respect, developed between the two.

The first popular Government of the State of Bombay did fare very well in Bombay State. It was a government which followed the Gandhian ethos in every possible way. It took up pressing issues like debt relief to peasants and improvement in the tone of administration and worked wholeheartedly with the welfare of the people uppermost in mind. Morarji in particular practised austerity in his public and private life. As a rule he usually travelled by 3rd or 2nd class by rail and seldom gave in to luxuries or pomp and show.

Prohibition was introduced in Bombay State, by the Kher ministry, and Dr Gilder, a Parsi, was the minister in charge. The Excise Commissioner Mr Knight was opposed to this. After the ministry demitted office in 1939, Mr Knight became

Advisor to the Governor and made a thorough inquiry into the implementation of the Prohibition in the state. He is said to have publicly stated that the Prohibition Policy had indeed been very successful, more so among the labour class.

In September 1939, Lord Linlithgow, the then Viceroy had unilaterally declared that India was at war with Germany without consulting the people of India or their elected governments. The Congress objected strongly to the declaration of war without prior consultation. The Congress Working Committee suggested that it would cooperate if there were a central Indian national government formed, and a commitment made to India's Independence after the war.

The government did not come up with any satisfactory response. Linlithgow could only offer to form a 'Consultative Committee' for advisory functions. Thus, Linlithgow refused the demands of the Congress. On 22 October 1939, all Congress ministries were called upon to tender their resignations. The Congress ministries resigned in October and November 1939, in protest against the Viceroy's action. After resigning Morarji went to Ahmedabad and busied himself in work relating to the Congress party.

The Individual Satyagraha was a movement first started by Mahatma Gandhi, in 1939, not as a mass movement to seek Independence but as a movement to affirm the right of speech. Non-violence was the watchword of this Individual Satyagraha. To this end the satyagrahis were carefully chosen. Acharya Vinobha Bhave was the first to court arrest when he spoke against the War, Jawaharlal Nehru the second and Brahma Dutt the third. Gandhi suspended this Individual Satyagraha in mid-1940, but later revived it in 1941. Morarji was amongst the many prominent leaders who courted arrest during the second phase of the satyagraha, the revived Individual Satyagraha. He was housed in Sabarmati Jail and later shifted to Yeravada Jail.

Morarji took an active part in the 'Quit India' movement of 1942. On 9 August 1942, Mahatma Gandhi, Morarji and many other Congress leaders were arrested and kept in the Yervada Jail. B.G. Kher was one of his companions in Jail. Another was Nuri, a friend of his, from whom he learnt Urdu during this jail term. During this term, Morarji also had the occasion to read the Koran and gain insights into Islam. Jail life helped him get acquainted with the real character of many of his companions housed there with him. Little did he know then that he would be sent to jail in independent India too! But more of that later.

The jail term ended in 1945 and Morarji's release coincided with the end of the Second World War. In 1946, a second ministry was formed by B.G. Kher, in which Morarji was the number two man holding the twin portfolios of Home and Revenue. Soon after, riots broke out in Bombay and Ahmedabad due to the surcharged communal atmosphere in the country at that time. In Ahmedabad Morarji was able to quickly bring the situation under control by moving around and being physically present in the disturbed areas for many hours and ensuring in his characteristic way that the police carried out their duty efficiently and effectively, without any bias. He also made sure that Section 144 was lifted and people could move about freely and discuss their problems with him. Thus, the situation was soon under control. Even in Bombay the situation was fast brought under control with similar efficient handling. During his tenure as Home Minister he was known for his determination to curb lawlessness wherever it erupted. The rank and file of the state police held him in high esteem as even a junior policemen could approach Morarji directly, if he felt he had suffered an injustice and present his case.

During the dark period of Partition Morarji did commendable work for the protection of minorities and refugees. Jawaharlal Nehru was highly impressed by Morarji's dedication to work and empathy for his fellow beings.

In January 1948 a person called Jagdish Prasad Jain contacted Morarji and B.G. Kher after Madan Lal, a refugee, had exploded a bomb at Gandhi's prayer meeting in an aborted assassination attempt. Jain told Morarji and Kher that a conspiracy was being hatched to kill the Mahatma and some others, apart from Madan Lal, may be involved in it. On the basis of this information and names and clues provided by him, Morarji called J.D. Nagarwala, the then DIG (CID) and asked him to take steps to immediately to arrest one Vishnu R. Karkare, a known Hindu Mahasabha activist who later was found to be one of the chief conspirators of Gandhi's assassination on 30 January 1948. Morarji also ordered that Veer Savarkar or Vinayak Damodar Savarkar, the legendary freedom fighter and past President of the Hindu Mahasabha, be put under unobtrusive surveillance. Savarkar was arrested after the assassination of Mahatma Gandhi and Morarji gave evidence against him. On being asked by Savarkar's lawyer as to why he had put Savarkar under surveillance, Morarji replied that if

Savarkar so desired he was willing to disclose some crucial facts about him. Savarkar's counsel promptly withdrew the question. While referring to Savarkar's involvement, Morarji had stated in the Bombay Legislative Council on 8 April, 1948, 'Savarkar's past services are more than offset by his present disservice.' As late as 12 July 2012, Swapan Dasgupta made a disclosure on television that L.K. Advani had told him that Morarji was convinced of Savarkar's complicity in Mahatma Gandhi's assassination, but he got away with it as the Judge acquitted him on the plea of lack of evidence as only the approver Digamber Bagde and a taxi driver had testified against him. (A.G. Noorani "Savarkar and Gandhi's Murder," *Frontline*, 22 Sep-05 Oct 2012). Sardar Patel had also expressed a similar opinion in a letter to Pandit Jawaharlal Nehru on 27 February 1948. The J.L. Kapur Commission appointed in the mid 1960s also collaborated Morarji's view based on the testimonies of Savarkar's secretary and bodyguard. But by then Savarkar was dead.

Chief Minister of Bombay (1952-1956)

After a successful tenure as Home Minister of the state, Morarji, being the senior-most Congress leader in the province as well as the senior-most minister, was tipped to take over from Chief Minister Kher, who was due to retire after the elections of 1952. He contested the elections from Bulsar, a seat considered safe from all points of view. Many Congress leaders and Ministers tasted defeat that year. People in India's nascent democracy had begun to realise the meaning of 'Free Vote.' Morarji's political opponent was a young Socialist Party activist Dr Amul Desai, who was a Medical Practitioner. When the results came in from Bulsar, people learnt with astounding surprise that the young Socialist doctor had defeated Morarji Desai, the powerful Home Minister of Bombay, by 19 votes, At first, it was announced that the margin of defeat was 219 and on a recount the margin was reduced to 19. Had another recount been done, probably Morarji's defeat would have been reversed into victory, but Morarji desisted from it as his opponent objected.

When analysed, it was apparent that the freak defeat had taken place because of the policy of Morarji's Revenue department, resulting in peasants voting against him. An

Independent candidate at Bulsar, Janardhan Desai, had also taken away 15000 votes, which might otherwise have gone to the Congress. Another factor was that Morarji was not able to spend enough time in Bulsar for campaigning.

When Morarji arrived in Bombay, at Juhu airport, flying in a state aircraft, his Private Secretary, Y.V. Tonpe, brought a message from Chief Minister Kher. Kher had said that Morarji should not give any statement to the press without consulting him first. Morarji had by then decided that he would resign from the government, as a mark of respect to the verdict of Bulsar.

However, when they met the next day, Kher would not hear of any talk of resignation. He was insistent that Morarji continue in office. He was of the firm opinion that one freak defeat should not come in the way of the planned arrangement for the Government of Bombay. Morarji, on the other hand, was of the view that he could do better work for the Congress from outside the government and said so to Kher. Kher countered this with the statement that Morarji's heading the new government would be more beneficial for the Congress party and would be in the interest of the organisation.

In addition to Kher, the Prime Minister Jawaharlal Nehru, and all the PCC Presidents in Bombay State, namely Bhausaheb Hirey for Maharashtra, S.K. Patil for Bombay, Nijalingappa for Karnataka and Kanjibhai Desai for Gujarat were in favour of Morarji heading the government, he being the ablest person available for the task. Thus, Morarji was unanimously elected leader of the Congress Legislature Party. He first became a member of the Legislative Council and after some months entered the Legislative Assembly after winning the bye-election from a labour constituency from Ahmedabad city, where he won by a large margin.

The Constitution of the Bombay Congress Legislature Party had to be amended as it provided that only a member of the Legislative Assembly could be its leader. Some newspapers like *The Times of India* criticised the decision, but it was just a case of the press being a little biased, as often happens in a democracy. It is an interesting point, that in the general election of 1957 when Morarjibhai stood as a candidate for Parliament, the Congress candidate at Bulsar, the relatively unknown Gopalji Desai, defeated the same Dr Amul Desai, of the Socialist Party, by a huge margin of 19,000 votes.

In forming his Cabinet, Morarji had to give due weightage to Maharashtra, being one of the Chief constituents of bilingual Bombay. Morarji was proceeding to Calcutta for the annual Congress Session. He sent word to Bhausaheb Hirey, the senior Congress leader from Maharashtra, that the cabinet formation could be discussed on the train to Calcutta. This was immediately reported in the Marathi press. Morarji naturally did not like this leaking of sensitive information. In the train, Hirey did not come to Morarji's compartment, so Morarji decided not to call him. It appeared that Hirey was deliberately being difficult. On his return to Bombay, Morarji told Hirey that the names being considered from Maharashtra were Hirey himself, Y.B. Chavan, who was then a junior legislator and who had earlier been Morarji's Parliamentary Secretary when he was Home Minister, Naik Nimbalkar, the ruler of Phaltan who had also been a Minister in

Kher's cabinet and G.D. Tapase, a reserved category candidate, who in later years was made a Governor by Morarji. Tapase had also been in Kher's cabinet.

Hirey agreed about himself and Chavan, but did not want the inclusion of Tapase and Nimbalkar. He wanted Morarji to bring in Kunte, another Maharashtrian. Morarji and Hirey both met Pandit Jawaharlal Nehru in Delhi and Panditji accepted Morarji's viewpoint. Maulana Azad, who also took part in the discussions, wanted to know why a Muslim name did not figure in the cabinet, to which Morarji said that Muslims would be there as Deputy Ministers to take care of minority interests.

On the Maulana offering to name a suitable Muslim, Morarji candidly replied that any such name could not be considered. He held on to the firm belief that the formation of the ministry was the Chief Minister's prerogative.

Morarji agreed to make Hirey's man, Kunte, the Speaker of the Assembly. Apart from Hirey, the other names for Maharashtra in the cabinet were Tapase, Chavan and Naik Nimbalkar as desired and decided by Morarji. In addition to Revenue, Morarji gave Hirey the portfolio of Agriculture as well.

Thus, Morarji formed his first Cabinet in Bombay State. Morarji's foremost trouble arose on the occasion of the presentation of the Budget, where his Finance Minister Jivraj Mehta had proposed an increase in Sales Tax netting a revenue of Rs. 10-11 crores.

Morarji came back from Delhi to Pune where the Assembly was then meeting to take stock of the situation as there was a threat of revolt in the Legislative Party. He immediately called a meeting of the Legislative Party and asked members to express their views frankly. After long discussions, Morarji made it clear that the members should decide what was best for the Party. The overwhelming verdict was in favour of the Sales Tax Bill to be introduced.

Thus, the step was brought about, after complete discussion and debate with the party fully supporting the government and agreeing to a move which was likely to be unpopular. Soon after, when Bhausaheb Hirey threatened to resign on some issue, Morarji called his bluff, by telling him that he was free to quit if he so desired. Never after that, did Hirey hold out a threat of leaving the ministry.

Once these initial teething troubles were over or rather successfully surmounted, Morarji was able to usher in a stable and effective government in Bombay State. Being an able administrator and a true democrat who firmly believed in the decentralisation of functioning, he made sure that he carried his ministry with him. The overall development of the state and welfare of the people was always his highest priority.

Some members of the press and other interested parties were unduly critical of his Prohibition Policy, which he had only implemented, like all other policies of the Cabinet, in the same firm way as any just administrator would. Morarji had always been a very humane person, though he was time and again misunderstood. More often than not, he had been projected in the media and other public fora as a stern, rigid and unyielding person without compassion or empathy, while the truth was just the reverse. He had a sharp wit and a keen sense of humour and was easily accessible to the common man. The kind of criticism he faced is something honest people in public life had to face and endure, their courage and fortitude put to test by such criticisms. Morarji, undaunted, lived by his convictions and principles in both his public and private life and remained unfazed by criticism to the end.

When some newspapers like *The Times of India* started a personalised campaign and mud-slinging attack on him on the Prohibition issue, Morarji promptly withdrew governmental advertising from *The Times of India.* Later when amicable relations were restored and the personal vendetta against Morarji was withdrawn by the newspaper, Morarji removed the ban and allowed governmental advertising to appear in the newspaper.

During his tenure in the State, he saw to it that administrative reforms were undertaken for the benefit and welfare of the community at large. The Public Distribution System was made to work effectively, so that most of the essential commodities were freely available to the people. In the field of Education, his ministry took steps to see that the mother tongue remained the medium of instruction in the State Boards, with Hindi as a compulsory language and English to be taught after the eighth standard. Morarji felt that a child's intellectual potential could be fully realised and developed only if the language spoken at home was the medium of instruction at school too.

On 15 December 1952, Potti Sriramalu died as a result of a fast undertaken to demand separate Statehood for Andhra which was then a part of the Madras Presidency. As a reaction and a fallout, widespread violence took place in the districts of Madras

State where Telugu-speaking people enjoyed a majority. On 18 December 1952, the Union Cabinet approved the formation of a separate Andhra State. In December 1953, the Centre appointed a Three-member commission under Justice Fazal Ali to go into the question of 'Reorganisation of States on Linguistic basis. Morarji was opposed to this move. He felt, and rightly so, that this would hamper the unity of the country and allow fissiparous tendencies to develop. But unfortunately, his was a minority voice as most others were in favour of such a move. In a letter to Prime Minister Nehru on 20 December 1952, he is reported to have stated:

> *'I must frankly confess to a feeling of distress at what appears to me to be a decision which is perhaps inevitable but taken under political pressure, a decision whose consequence it would be difficult to foresee. I venture to think if the main resolution of the Congress on linguistic provinces had been held in abeyance for ten years in order that the process of consolidation of the welfare activities of the State Governments may not be disturbed ... This may in turn set in motion political forces which it would be difficult to control or satisfy without injury to the welfare work that immediately lies ahead of us.*
>
> *Please forgive me if I am adding to your worries by raising a discordant note. I am doing it with the heaviest of hearts as I consider it disloyalty to you to hold back my view which goes counter to yours especially when I strongly feel that the course you propose to take will be highly disastrous*

and will harm the work of building up a united India to a considerable extent and will also hold up the execution of the Five Year Plan in the States concerned.'

The State Reorganisation Commission presented its report in 1955. According to it Vidarbha was to separate from Bombay State, as it had been a part of Central India, Maharashtra and Gujarat would remain in Bombay State, and Karnataka would go to the then Mysore State. When the report was discussed before the AICC it was decided that Bombay City, Maharashtra and Gujarat should be three separate states. Morarji was opposed to this, but, since the majority members as well as Nehru were in favour of it, it had to be accepted. However, this could not be implemented at the time, as events following the decision proved.

Politicians at times get driven by ideology to an extent where logic takes a back seat. Morarji's commitment to homespun khadi is one example. Without doubt it has provided employment to many but development of other industries would also provide enough if systematically done. In a radio speech in Bombay as Chief Minister he once said, 'If our national economy is to be sound we must develop intense patriotism for Indian goods especially khadi and other products of cottage industry.' Many people felt that with the attainment of Independence the relevance of khadi which was basically a tool to boycott British and other foreign goods had ended. However, it must be remembered that Gandhiji had also not given up advocacy of khadi after India became free. The jury is out on this question of considerable importance but taking a middle path would be of relevance in the fast developing world of today. This is not to say that one should in any way discourage handicrafts as a provider of employment to the masses as well as representing Indian products in its unique way. I doubt if Morarji would have disagreed with the changing times without forgetting his commitment to khadi.

Digressing a little here the author would like to mention an interesting incident relating to this period. The late D.F. Karaka, (also known as Dosu Karaka) editor of *Current* weekly, had written an interesting biography of Morarji Desai titled *Morarji* in 1965. He had described his first meeting with Morarji when he went for an interview of Morarji in 1956 when the issue of States Reorganisation was a hot topic. When Karaka arrived at *Corsley* on Malabar Hill, which was Morarji's official residence, he was struck by the simplicity of the house. He had expected a Chief Minister of a premier state like Bombay to live in greater splendour but, as he himself put it, this was probably because, 'I did not know Morarji so well then.'

Karaka and his weekly had in the past not had cordial relations with Morarji. In later years he was to develop a great regard and affection for Morarji, of which he gives ample expression to in his biography of the master statesman. He says that he was determined to show the utmost courtesy in the interview as it was he (Karaka) who had requested for it and Morarji had agreed to grant it.

As Morarji would be leaving Bombay, either when the State was reorganised, or after the next General Election due in early 1957, Karaka opened the interview by asking whether Morarji knew what his next assignment would be; would it be in the Union Cabinet, or as some believed, would he take over the newly formed Gujarat State. Morarji indicated that he had no idea and that the decision would be that of Prime Minister Nehru. 'My own idea would be to have no office of any kind,' Morarji said after a pause and indicated that he meant getting into active public service without holding any office.

Morarji then went on to say that he would like Karaka to understand him. That was 'much more important.' Both of them then had an open straightforward talk, which formed the basis for an enduring lifelong relationship. Morarji explained that his main urge in life was 'self-realisation' in the manner of the sages of ancient India. 'I am in politics only because I believe in an active life,' he said. 'For instance, after years of trying, I have finally been able to conquer anger.' All this had its effect on Karaka and impressed him tremendously. Karaka felt that Morarji's remarks certainly commanded respect. Morarji, he was convinced, was an extraordinary person, one who dared to bare his soul and be open, even while conversing with one of his harshest critics.

The interview then turned to international Affairs. On the issue of Communism, Morarji said, 'I am opposed to the violence embedded in Communism. I am opposed to the whole Communist philosophy because it is based on violence and I am opposed to any form of totalitarianism.'

Then Karaka brought up the burning issue of Reorganisation of States. Morarji felt that it would not be appropriate to comment on this delicate issue at that point of time. The next topic was on the agitation to free Goa from Portuguese rule.

'Basically, it is the Goans who have to achieve it and we have to help them, consistent with the principles we follow in our national and international policies,' was Morarji's sage and solid remark.

Karaka tried to steer the conversation around to the future, but Morarji did not let him veer towards that ambiguous topic. This was because of Morarji's unshakeable faith in God and the power of destiny. The interview ended with Karaka asking a question on Defence preparedness and the Defence Budget in general. Morarji felt that the country could not afford to be slack in its readiness and had to be ready and able to repulse any attack from Pakistan. When Karaka referred to the danger of China attacking India, Morarji replied in the negative which goes to show that both political leaders of that time and the public at large did not regard China as a potential enemy and just six years later India was subjected to a full scale invasion from that country. Karaka says he asked the question because the talk at that time was that if Morarji went to the Centre, Defence was the portfolio he was likely to get. Thus ended the first interview D.F. Karaka had with Morarji on 23 April, 1956.

The Samyukta Maharashtra Agitation subsequently took an ugly turn as its leaders were very much against the decision of the

AICC to keep Bombay city out of Maharashtra. Riots broke out in Bombay city and things were getting out of control. Morarji gave proper instructions to the police and told them to take strict action where required.

Police firing had to be resorted to and some 70 to 80 people were killed. Had this not been done, a terrible situation would have developed in Bombay city with many more casualties and severe damage to property. Nehru had told Morarji that if necessary, the army could also be deployed to control the situation. But Morarji felt that since restoring law and order was the primary job of the police, it would be bad for its morale if the army was called in. Moreover, there would probably have been more casualties if the army had been brought in. Not only that, it would have set a bad precedent for the future. Nehru concurred with the views expressed by Morarji.

The riots were soon brought under control and peace was restored in Bombay city. However, by July 1956, it was decided by the central leadership that Bombay State should not be divided as suggested earlier. It would now be a bigger bilingual state.

The reaction in Gujarat to this decision was hostile. It had earlier been happy at the prospect of getting separate statehood. Violence broke out in Ahmadabad and continued, dangerously, with the Maha Gujarat Movement raging on. Morarji decided that he should take an initiative at his own level now. He decided to proceed on a fast akin to Gandhiji's practice, to atone for the violence and to restore normalcy in Ahmadabad and Gujarat. Already, quite a few lives had been lost in police firing and more use of force alone would have led to a deterioration of law and order. Being a Gandhian, Morarji felt that an indefinite fast would wean citizens away from violence and bring about the normalcy and love for a peaceful life which Gujarat was known for.

He had even informed Pandit Nehru that he was willing to resign the Chief Ministership in order to undertake the fast. But, this was not required as Nehru gave his consent to it. Thus, in August 1956, Morarji went on a fast at Ahmedabad, which went on for quite a few days. The Congress President U.N. Dhebar was present with him throughout the period of a fast. After eight days of his fast, on 26 August 1956, the Congress organised a public meeting at the Lal Darwaja maidan in Ahmedabad. Six to seven thousand people gathered at the meeting which Morarji addressed for about forty-five minutes.

A small group of lumpen elements kept pelting the people on the stage with stones all through the duration of the meeting. Even Morarji's wife was injured. But, as Morarji had given the police strict instructions not to take action against these juveniles, the stoning continued throughout the meeting, with impunity.

After the meeting, listening to the pleas of a great number of people, Morarji broke his fast. Had he not undertaken this fast, the violence would have escalated and spread to other areas of Gujarat and a nasty situation would have arisen. The violence in Ahmedabad soon petered out after this meeting.

The larger Bombay State was to come into effect from 1 Nov 1956. Morarji had decided that he would not like to head it and would like someone else to take on the responsibility as he had been in government for 10 years.

A large number of his colleagues as well as Prime Minister Nehru felt that he should continue in Bombay State, a proposition Morarji was willing to consider provided he was elected unanimously as leader of the Congress Legislature Party.

However, since Bhausaheb Hirey was bent on putting up his name as a candidate, on the day of the leadership election, Morarjibhai withdrew his name which had been proposed and instead supported the name of Y.B. Chavan who was at that time the junior-most cabinet minister in Bombay. In the contest Chavan overwhelmingly trounced Hirey, thus, proving Morarji's hold over the Congress Legislature Party.

Pandit Nehru had by now made it clear to Morarji that his services would be required for the Central Cabinet, if he was not staying on to lead the Bombay team. A leader as senior and experienced as him had to be taken in the Central or State government machinery and could not be allowed to remain as just a party worker. Earlier during discussions, Nehru had made it clear that he wanted Morarji to take over the Finance Ministry. He had kept the portfolio with him since the resignation of C.D. Deshmukh earlier in the year.

However, during the intervening period, T.T. Krishnamachari was moved into the Finance Ministry as the Foreign Exchange situation had deteriorated. When Nehru told Morarji that it was a temporary arrangement, Morarji replied that it did not matter to him and that he, Nehru, could make any arrangement he thought proper and in the larger interest of the nation.

In Nehru's Cabinet (1956-1963)

When Morarji arrived in Delhi, Nehru asked him to choose between Defence and Commerce & Industry as those were the portfolios available at that time. Morarji reiterated that he was equally comfortable with any portfolio that was allotted to him. He, however, went on to say that if he took charge of the Defence Ministry, he would not be able to take an active part in day-to-day politics. It was his view that a Defence Minister should not be actively or intensely involved in politics, so as to adhere to the discipline and morale of the Armed Forces.

Nehru felt that at that crucial juncture, Morarji's active presence in politics was a key factor and was essential for the Congress. Therefore, on 14 November, 1956, Morarji was sworn in as Minister for Commerce & Industry in the Union Cabinet.

He was designated No.4 in the Union Cabinet, after the Prime Minister, G.B. Pant and Maulana Azad. During the period he held charge of the Commerce & Industry portfolio he made sure that he did his best for the development of small scale and cottage industries. He also saw to it that the nascent Indian industry flourished and developed, by ensuring that it did not face undue competition from more developed foreign industrial set-ups by putting necessary trade and tariff restrictions on such foreign industrial set-ups planning to invest in India or set up industries and the like. He saw to it that luxury items were cut as much as possible from Indian imports to save on foreign exchange, the reserves of which were low and availability scarce. During the period in this ministry he shifted his office from North Block to the new Udyog Bhavan which had become ready for occupation in 1957.

Around September, 1957, the Mundhra scandal broke out in Parliament regarding certain loans taken by a businessman, Haridas Mundhra, from the LIC. The Mundhra scandal exposed the nexus between the bureaucracy, stock market speculators and small corrupt businessmen. It brought to light the rifts between Nehru and his son-in-law Feroze Gandhi. Feroze Gandhi had played a leading role in the exposure. Justice M.C. Chagla was asked to inquire into this and he recorded certain strictures in his report against the Finance Minister T.T. Krishnamachari. Accordingly, Krishnamachari resigned as Finance Minister in February, 1958.

A meeting took place between Nehru, Morarji and G.B. Pant. Nehru and Pant were of the opinion that Morarji should take up the Finance portfolio. Morarji felt that Pant had handled Finance very well in U.P. and would be able to do so equally well at the Centre. Pant was of the view that considering his age and health he would not be able to handle the Finance Ministry. His health did not permit him to travel abroad as frequently as would be needed. Morarji had clashed with Krishnamachari on the working of the Finance Ministry and now felt that he might take it ill. But, since Nehru was insistent, he agreed.

Taking charge of the Union Finance Ministry in March 1958, Morarji undoubtedly had a challenging task ahead of him. Even though Nehru had presented the Budget during the brief period that he held the Finance portfolio, it fell to Morarji's lot to pilot the Finance Bill in parliament and reply to all the questions regarding it. Deficit financing was on the high side when he took over.

The Ministers of State who were under him were B. Gopala Reddy (later Governor of Uttar Pradesh), and B.R. Bhagat (who was later Speaker of the Lok Sabha). The Deputy Finance Minister was Tarakeshwari Sinha. Morarji de-centralised the working of the Ministry among his junior ministers and secretaries and ensured that the system worked smoothly and efficiently.

In 1958, after straightening out things in the Finance Ministry, Morarji left for the Commonwealth Finance Ministers' Conference at Montreal, Canada, stopping en route at London and Washington. This was his first visit abroad.

The visit was important and crucial for the Indian economy. India needed foreign aid at that time as it was facing difficulties in the implementation of the Second Five Year Plan. Foreign exchange for the three steel plants at Bhilai, Rourkela and Durgapur was imperative and inescapable. During this period India's Defence expenditure had also increased substantially and necessary provision had to be made to increase and augment the Defence Budget.

In his discussions in London with Prime Minister Macmillan and Chancellor of the Exchequer Eastcote Armey, Morarji was able to press home the requirement for deferring aid on easier terms. This was absolutely necessary and inescapable for the timely and efficient execution of India's development plans.

During his London trip, he was interviewed by a group of four journalists on television, one of whom was a BBC correspondent Mrs Katherine Dove. The interview progressed very well and Morarji managed to put the interviewers who were posing awkward questions in a bit of a tight spot with his sharp, incisive, forthright answers. The interview was very successful in putting India's viewpoints across to Great Britain and its people. Lord Mountbatten congratulated Morarji for handling the interview superbly and becoming a 'TV Star' overnight.

In the United States, Morarji had fruitful talks with Eugene Black, the then President of the World Bank, Douglas Dillon, the then Economic Advisor to the US Government and Robert Anderson, then Secretary of the Treasury ensuring that the US government and the financial institutions proffering aid understood and appreciated India's needs and compulsions better. While at New York, he again had a very successful interview with the editors of *Time-Life* group. While on this trip, he visited Vernon and had some informal chitchat with the sightseers there. On the whole, he gave the Americans an impression of being a very affable person.

Morarji wound up his foreign trip with the Commonwealth Finance Ministers' Conference in Montreal, Canada. On the whole it was his efforts which saved the Indian Economy from the serious difficulties that threatened its health and functioning at that time.

The late 1950s and early '60s were a period of momentous political turmoil for India and the subcontinent. Morarji, as Finance Minister, was naturally affected by it. It would be in the fitness of things, to narrate events during this period in chronological order.

Towards the end of 1959, the proposal for the division of the bilingual Bombay State was brought up. As earlier (in 1956), Morarji was opposed to it as he felt that the concept of linguistic states was against the goal of national integration. However, Morarji found that the majority of his colleagues including Prime Minister Nehru and the Chief Minister of Bombay, Yashwantrao Balwantrao Chavan were in favour of it. So he had to let it pass, even though he made it clear to his colleagues that his was a dissent vote and that he was not in favour of it. Thus, on 1 May, 1960 the separate states of Maharashtra and Gujarat came into being.

Towards the end of 1959 Morarji attended IMF meetings at Washington and the Commonwealth Finance Ministers' Conference at London with short stopovers in Switzerland and France. It was during this visit, during a TV interview at New York, the interviewer said that he wanted to introduce Morarji as India's future Prime Minister. Morarji, immediately objected as he felt that it was improper and indecorous. When the interviewer insisted that it was his right and privilege to word his introduction the way he wanted to, Morarji countered that as the interviewee he too had equal rights to leave the interview and proceeded to walk out. The interviewer immediately understood that Morarji was firm and meant business and desisted from his proposed introduction.

Morarji visited Russia in 1960 on the invitation of Khrushchev. Actually, he had first met Khrushchev in 1955, when he was the Chief Minister of Bombay, during the time that Bulganin and Khrushchev had made a whirlwind tour of India. At that time, probably as a result of Morarji's frank conversation with them, they did not ask him to visit Russia. However, when Khrushchev came to India in 1960, he insisted repeatedly and sincerely that Morarji should come to Russia. He conveyed this desire to Nehru as well.

A few months after Khrushchev's visit, the Russian Ambassador met Morarji and tried to convince him that the visit would definitely prove of beneficial to India. Yielding to the persistent requests, Morarji planned a trip covering West Germany, Egypt, Yugoslavia, Poland and Czechoslovakia, along with the USSR.

His visit was certainly very fruitful as he was able to get an additional aid of 500 million roubles for the Third Five Year Plan. It so happened that President Rajendra Prasad was also in the Soviet Union at that time. When certain Indian media persons who were accompanying the President asked the Soviet Vice-Premier Mikoyan as to what help the Soviet Union was going to give India, he said that the Indian Finance Minister had not asked for any help.

Using this comment to his advantage, Morarji, when he met Mikoyan for talks promptly brought up the issue. He referred to Mikoyan's comment to the journalists that help had not been sought for and said that he was making a specific request with regard to aid for the Third Five Year Plan of India. Soon after, an additional 500 million roubles aid was announced.

With Khrushchev, Morarji had an interesting discussion during this trip. Khrushchev brought the discussion around to God and religion. And being a true believer, Morarji put across his views emphatically and unambiguously. Khrushchev quipped, 'God has told me not to believe in Him.' Morarji's quick-witted repartee was that he was quite satisfied with the reply as Khrushchev had admitted to the existence of God; not only that, he had affirmed that he was in direct communication with God. Khrushchev was effectively silenced and did not dwell any more on the topic. Morarji could get on quite well with Khrushchev and his visit was highly appreciated by the latter.

Towards the end of 1961, the Liberation of Goa from Portuguese rule by the Indian Army took place. Morarji was not in agreement with the decision as he felt this was against India's well-established policy of finding peaceful solutions to problems of this nature. Some people felt that Defence Minister Krishna Menon had taken the Goa action to get over the opposition for his election from the North Bombay Lok Sabha seat during the forthcoming 1962 General Elections.

During the period 1961-62, Morarji had two meetings with President Kennedy, who had genuine interest in India and Indians and was able to understand and appreciate Morarji's line of thinking.

In 1961 Pandit Govind Ballabh Pant who was Home Minister in Nehru's Cabinet since 1955, passed away. It had been the tradition that the person who was No.2 in the Cabinet would be the Deputy Leader of the Parliamentary Party. However, Nehru dodged the issue and declared that henceforth two members from both Houses of Parliament, who were not ministers, would be appointed as Deputy Leaders of the Party. Earlier to that the leftist group in the Congress urged the then Railway Minister Jagjivan Ram to contest for the Deputy Leadership. Ultimately Nehru's proposal for two non-ministerial candidates for Deputy Leaders was accepted even though there was a controversy of how the resolution was passed in the Parliamentary Party – a member had called for a division which was ignored by Nehru at the meeting. Morarji felt that it was a deliberate ploy by Nehru to reduce his political stature in the Cabinet as he wanted Indira Gandhi to ultimately succeed him. She had become the Congress President in 1959.

Shortly after, occurred the well-known and well-documented misadventure of the Indo-Chinese war of 1962, during which the Indian armed forces were outnumbered and outgunned, resulting in loss of territory and prestige. Due to a strong demand of the Congress Parliamentary Party combined with the pressing outcry of public opinion, for the ouster of Krishna Menon from the Cabinet, several Congress leaders including Morarji, told Nehru that he could not ignore the demand and it was very necessary for him to see the writing on the wall. Krishna Menon was accordingly dropped from the Cabinet in November, 1962.

As an aftermath of the Chinese aggression, Morarji enforced the Gold Control Order in January, 1963. This basically dealt with the curbing of gold smuggling. It also brought into force the ban on the manufacture and possession of gold greater in value than 14 carats. The 1963-64 Budget had to be a harsh one, in the larger interest of the nation. Defence resources had to be augmented to ensure that the nation could effectively meet future challenges and not be found wanting in the sphere of defence of the nation.

During that year (1963-64) the Defence Budget was increased to ₹868 crores from ₹395 crores the previous year. Morarji also introduced the Compulsory Deposit Scheme which in the long run was beneficial to the middle-class wage earner.

However, he had to face a lot of criticism as a result of these stringent measures and far-sighted schemes, but Morarji was unfazed and bore the brunt of the criticism stoically. Some Communist leaders who had, in private, welcomed the decision, now publically joined the chorus of opposition. Morarji, who had never shirked standing up for anything that was in the public and national interest, no matter how much criticism it might bring, took this disapproval and denigration in his stride with his usual stoicism.

His years as Finance Minister give one an insightful peek into Morarji's routine which was to remain unchanged all through his life. An early riser by habit, he would generally finish his yoga exercises between 5:00 to 5:30 am. After this he would have a light breakfast of milk or curds and by 7:00 am be ready to receive the first visitor, utilising that time to simultaneously spin khaddar on portable charkhas, a Gandhian activity followed by many of the Mahatma's followers. (Many a times the author has been in conversation with him during his morning spinning routine and had found it an interesting and rewarding experience to watch Morarji spin the yarn deftly while paying full attention to the conversation). During later years, his main meal for the day comprised milk, cottage cheese, fruits and dry fruits taken around 9:45 am. He would then proceed with his office routine: meeting visitors, attending to work, conferences, meetings and the usual work a Minister had to do during the course of the day. Back from office would be the time for his evening walk and meeting various people. Around sunset, say around 6:45 pm would be the time for his evening meal following which he would retire for the day, unless on tour or due to some official engagement as a Minister or later as the Prime Minister. American journalist Welles Hangen (who died in the Vietnam War) in his well known book *After Nehru Who?* says this of Morarji as Finance Minister, 'Whenever I call on him at his office or home I have difficulty in spotting him behind his mountain of files. If his attention wanders during our conversation, he may pick up one of his folders and begin scanning it with pursed lips and a look of Olympian resignation. Usually, however, I find him a good listener and what is more important an articulate exponent of his own ideas.' Hangen, in this quote, does bring out the essentials of Morarji Desai: Serious about the work and yet attentive to his visitor. The bureaucrat in him did probably never die, and he continued to follow his regimen with files which he acquired in the Provincial Civil Service under the British. It was the author's experience too in his numerous interactions with Morarji that he would be willing to discuss any subject and if free he would not hesitate to go into the intricate details of the topic being discussed.

Hangen, in his book published in 1963, a year before Nehru passed away, said he expected a 'Stop Desai movement after Nehru goes.' He was proved right in this as the following chapters would show, but he was wrong in one observation in his book: 'Desai's Hindu traditionalism is not likely to make him more sympathetic to Pakistan than Nehru or (Krishna) Menon were.' Morarji as Prime Minister did have fairly good terms with Pakistan. In fact he is the only leader from India to have received Pakistan's highest civilian honour: 'Nishan-e-Pakistan.' Hangen's comments are an example of how journalists at times have fixed views in their perceptions of leaders. However, it must be said that Hangen, in his book, gives a fair picture of Morarji as an administrator of ability.

In May-June 1963, Messrs Atulya Ghosh, S. Nijalingappa, N. Sanjeeva Reddy, U.S. Malaya and K. Kamaraj had a meeting at Tirupati during which certain discussions took place regarding the Party Presidentship and the successor to Nehru. This was one of the first meetings of that Syndicate. At that time the three parliamentary by-elections in Amroha, Farukhabad and Rajkot had gone to the opposition and this was alarming for the Congress.

It was at this time that Kamaraj, the Chief Minister of Madras brought forward a 'Plan' which according to him was designed to help in brightening the image and working of the Congress Party. It envisaged asking the party's senior leaders to quit the ministries at the Centre and the States and engage in active work for the Congress Organisation. Earlier, Biju Patnaik had also spoken to Nehru on these lines. Morarji suggested, at that time, that better results could be achieved if the size of the ministries at the Centre and States was pruned to effect economy in government spending and cut down wasteful expenditure.

However, Morarji's views did not prevail. All the ministers at the Centre and the Chief Ministers of the States sent in their resignations to Prime Minister Nehru. Morarji had made it clear time and again that he had never had any desire for any office and he readily sent in his resignation from the Cabinet.

Soon, Nehru informed the Working Committee that he would be accepting the resignations of the central cabinet ministers Morarji Desai, S.K. Patil, Jagjivan Ram, Lal Bahadur Shastri and B. Gopala Reddy and the chief ministers B.N. Jha from Bihar, Kamaraj from Madras and C.B. Gupta from Uttar Pradesh. Bakshi Ghulam Mohammad of J&K also resigned even though he, as a member of the National Conference, was not bound to do so. Morarji felt that his leaving Jammu & Kashmir at that juncture did not augur well for the State and in later years hampered the cause of development there.

As a disciplined soldier of the party, Morarji accepted the Kamaraj Plan even though it had diabolical overtones in view of the succession which was to take place on Nehru's death nine months later.

Party Worker and Deputy Prime Minister (1964-1969)

At the AICC Session at Bhubaneshwar, in January 1964, Morarji staunchly defended the Kamraj Plan. This was an exemplary manifestation of his avowed principle of party before politics and loyalty to the Congress despite personal biases. It was at the Bhubaneshwar Session that Prime Minister Nehru suffered a stroke. He recovered, but his health was never the same. It may be of some interest to readers that Morarji felt that Nehru would have been a far greater person and leader than he was had he believed in God. This distance from God made Nehru a solitary person despite his great hold on the masses of India. (D.F. Karaka, *Morarji*, Times of India Press, 1965).

On 27 May 1964 Prime Minister Nehru passed away on his return from a short holiday in Dehradun. As the nation mourned the death of one of its illustrious sons, it was naturally concerned as to who would lead the nation in the future. Gulzarilal Nanda, the senior-most Minister in the Nehru Cabinet, became the acting Prime Minister during the interregnum.

Kamaraj, as President of the Congress, took charge of all the Chief Ministers and important Congress leaders who had assembled for Nehru's funeral and felt there was a need to evolve a consensus within the Congress Parliamentary Party (CPP) regarding the new leader. Morarji opposed this as he felt that it would be a body-blow to the democratic functioning of the Congress. However, in view of the paramount necessity to maintain unity in the Congress, Morarji withdrew from the contest and let Lal Bahadur Shastri, by manipulated consensus, be elected leader of the CPP and in the capacity become the second Prime Minister of India. Kuldip Nayar was heading the United News of India (UNI) when Shastri succeeded Nehru. On the day after Nehru's death Nayar visited Morarji's residence on Tygaraj Marg. Morarji was unavailable but Nayar met his son Kantibhai who had quit his business ventures earlier in the year to work for his father. Kantibhai called Nayar 'Shastri's man' and asked Nayar to tell Shastri to opt out of the contest. He was flourishing a list of MPs who were supporting Morarji. Nayar claimed he told Kanti that he was merely a journalist out to gauge both the camps and not to take sides. Nayar then went on to interview Shastri whom he found reticent. He filed an article with the UNI, which was carried by most national dailies on their front page the next day, in which he wrote 'Morarji Desai was the first to throw in his hat in the ring for the leadership contest.' The article also went on to add that Shastri was in denial mode and not taking a clear position on the leadership issue. The thrust of the piece was such that it gave a bad image to Morarji Desai as an over ambitious person. Nayar said that this news item probably caused Morarji a hundred votes of parliamentarians. He got this impression when Shastri told him shortly after it was published, 'No more stories now, the game is over.' Morarji never forgave him for that article, Nayar remarked, when he went to congratulate him after he finally became Prime Minister and said to him, 'Morarjibhai you must be having a lot of problems to tackle,' Morarji replied, 'Yes. There would have been fewer problems if you had allowed me to become Prime Minister in 1964.' He remembered the story years later. All this goes to show the dexterous nature of Indian politics and the behind-the-scene politicking and bickering.

Lal Bahadur Shastri called Morarji and asked him to join the Cabinet, but with the stipulation that Gulzarilal Nanda would have to be No. 2, as he had been acting Prime Minister on Nehru's death, and Morarji could be No. 3 in the Cabinet. Morarji made it clear that as he had been No. 2 in Nehru's Cabinet, before he quit under the Kamaraj Plan and Nanda had been his junior, he could not accept this condition; it was an insult to him. Assuring Shastri of his co-operation from outside, he declined to accept any ministerial berth.

During the years 1964-65, being out of office, Morarji was able to undertake extensive tours throughout India. He also gave speeches at functions organised at various venues on burning issues facing the nation. At the AICC Session at Bangalore on 25 July, 1965, a resolution was brought in to give a second term of office to Kamaraj as Congress President. In order to achieve this, an amendment was brought into the Congress Constitution as according to it the AICC president could hold office only for one term.

Morarji opposed this amendment, for he felt, and rightly so, that in such crucial matters, no matter what the stature of an individual might be or whatever his importance to the party, a change in the Constitution of the party organisation to accommodate him was incorrect and unethical. It was against democratic principles and all the values that the Congress stood for. In a landmark speech before the AICC he articulated his views. Describing it as a 'Question of Conscience,' he made it clear that if the Congress lost its hold over the people the country would suffer and the quality of public life in the country had to be kept up.

Unfortunately, the amendment was brought in and the exception of giving a second term of office to Kamaraj was made. The democratic functioning of the Congress was being slowly eroded with moves such as this. However, as a loyal Congressman, Morarji co-operated with the Shastri government, by not saying anything publicly against its functioning. During the Indo-Pak war of September, 1965, Morarji gave a speech on All India Radio on 8 September, 1965. In November-December 1965, he represented India at the Asian Commonwealth Parliamentary Association Conference, at Wellington, New Zealand.

During this conference, Morarji made a very clear speech on the Kashmir issue after the Pakistan delegate raised it. He traced in a very lucid manner the historical background of the Kashmir issue. All the facts right from the time of Jinnah's unsuccessful visit in 1937-38, and again in 1947 till the recent aggression of 1965 were covered in his speech. Morarji mentioned how the people of Kashmiri had supported the National Conference so overwhelmingly for merger with India in 1947 and how the raiders sent by Jinnah in October 1947 were repelled. The speech Morarji gave was highly appreciated by all other delegates. The other members of the Indian delegation were Prof. N.G. Ranga, Swaminathan, S.M. Krishna and a lady doctor MLA from Bombay. Morarji also stopped en route at Sydney, where he met Sir Robert

Menzies, the Prime Minister of Australia, whom he had known earlier. Sir Robert was impressed with Morarji's explanation on the Kashmir issue and he readily accepted India's viewpoint.

Sir Robert Menzies hosted a luncheon in Morarji's honour where all his Ministers were present. He spoke very highly of Morarji Desai, during his speech at the lunch. Morarji who believed in nature cure and had never taken any injection since 1915 was exempted from vaccination. Australia and New Zealand have very strict laws in regard to vaccinations and this was the first time that vaccination was waived and an exception made for a visitor to these countries.

Madhu Limaye, the eminent Socialist Parliamentarian, recalled once that during his exile from government under the Kamaraj regime, Morarji came to his rescue in parliament when Congressmen constantly heckled him, 'Meet logic and argument with logic and argument, not by mere shouting and heckling,' Morarji is reported to have chided them.

Whilst on this period it would be quite appropriate to quote a passage written by Morarji in 1965-66, something that is very relevant in the national context even during the present times.

> 'Economic swaraj can only be achieved by mobilising real resources and investing in such industries as would accelerate the pace towards a self-sustaining economy. For this, the first thing we have to do is to cut down all low priority investments and expenditures, to make a determined effort to live within our means. This is absolutely necessary to maintain the health of the economy and to keep inflationary pressures in check.

> This is a situation where the only way out for us is the path of austerity. In government administration, in public corporations, in companies in the private sector and more important, in the personal lives of the privileged segment of our population, a determined spirit of austerity should inform all activities. Unless this is done, and done ruthlessly, the problem of resource mobilisation for both development and defence would not be tackled adequately. We are in that stage of national history when a little inadequacy in our endeavour may prove fatal. Today, resource mobilisation through austerity is the highest form of patriotism. Anything less may not do.'

The stress on 'Defence' in the above paragraph is important as Defence is the very basis of our sovereignty. Morarji had always felt that Defence should occupy a pride of place in our national priorities.

After Lal Bahadur Shastri's untimely demise, in Taskhent, Gulzarilal Nanda again became the acting Prime Minister. The Syndicate now put up Mrs Indira Gandhi to be the leader of Congress Parliamentary Party (CPP), as they felt that only she could defeat Morarji. They felt that Morarji would be too strong to control. This had been their consideration in 1964 also. Feelings that they could exercise control over Mrs Gandhi were belied within six to seven months, even more so after the devaluation of the Rupee on 6 June 1966.

Morarji insisted on a contest this time. It was essential to maintain the internal democratic functioning of the Congress.

During the days immediately after Shastri's demise, Jagjivan Ram initially supported Morarji for the leadership, but went over to the other side once he realised that they were in a stronger position. All Morarji did was to ring up the MPs to canvass for his candidature, whereas Kamaraj had the Chief Ministers issue an appeal for Mrs Gandhi.

The CPP Leadership election took place on 19 January, 1966. Morarji gave Mrs Gandhi a tough fight. Even though he lost he polled 165 votes. Incidentally, this was the only contest for the leadership of the Congress Parliamentary Party which had ever taken place to date.

Before Lal Bahadur Shastri's demise, he had sounded Morarji about the Chairmanship of the Administrative Reforms Commission which he had requested him to take up. As it turned out, Morarji took up this charge after Shastri's demise. The Commission was able to do useful work during his chairmanship which lasted about a year.

During the 1967 General Elections the Congress returned to power a badly mauled party. Many prominent members of the Syndicate, among them S.K. Patil, Atulya Ghosh and Kamaraj himself had been defeated in the elections. Various SVD (Samyukta Vidhayak Dal) Governments had been formed by the opposition parties in the Hindi-belt. In Tamil Nadu, the DMK had wrested power from the Congress.

Morarji had declared that he would stand for leadership of the CPP, after the 1967 elections, but he later withdrew in the interest of party unity as the majority of the Congress in the Lok Sabha was very thin. Morarji, at that time, was not inclined to accept any position in the new government. But since most of his senior colleagues in the party were of the view that he should join the Cabinet as Deputy Prime Minister, in order to maintain the stability and unity of the party and the government, he agreed. Mrs Gandhi had also requested him to do so.

Morarji was of the opinion that he should be given charge of the Home Ministry, if he were to be effective as Deputy Prime Minister. However, Mrs Gandhi insisted on giving him Finance and he took up the assignment in the interest of keeping the party together. Before the oath taking ceremony a meeting took place between Morarji and Indira Gandhi in which Yashwantrao Chavan and Jagjivan Ram, both senior cabinet ministers, were present, during which the powers and functions of the Deputy Prime Minister were discussed. As to the suggestion that the Deputy Prime Minister could give instructions and orders to the other members of the Cabinet, Morarji replied that the Deputy Prime Minister could certainly render advice to Ministers but not issue orders. (This was a bit ironic as some years later both Chavan and Jagjivan Ram became Deputy Prime Ministers in two different ministries).

Morarji did not like the cross examination and made it clear to Mrs Gandhi. She pacified him and said it should be taken in the right spirit and he should not let such things stand in the way of his joining the Cabinet. Later on Kamaraj also pressurised him to join the Cabinet as the majority in parliament was quite thin and his not joining would send a stronger message of instability within the party.

Consequently, in March 1967, Morarji returned to take over Finance, the portfolio that he had left in August, 1963. In May 1967, he presented the Budget for 1967-68, which had been delayed due to the General Elections. The economy was not in a good shape as 1966-67 had been a drought year and the rupee had been devalued in June, 1966. The Budget was both growth-oriented as well as aimed to put the country on a more stable footing economically.

In May 1967 a discussion took place in the Congress Working Committee regarding the nationalisation of banks. Morarji was of the view that social control of banks was a better proposition as this could be done through the Reserve Bank of India and could achieve the desired results by making the banks follow people-oriented policies of banking so that money was made more easily available to the common man. Morarji went on to inform the Working Committee that the scheme should be allowed to function for two years and if it did not work satisfactorily, he would himself bring about a proposal for nationalisation. This proposal was endorsed by the AICC at Jabalpur in 1968.

Morarji called a meeting of the Chairmen of various banks to bring about the implementation of the scheme which was done from May-June 1968. The law with regard to this was passed in February, 1969.

In August 1967 Morarji paid a visit to Japan on the invitation of Prime Minister Sato. He was highly impressed by the discipline and patriotism of the Japanese. He also had a stopover at Hong Kong while returning to Delhi. Later in September 1967, Morarji stopped over at London en route to Rio-de-Janeiro to attend the World Bank and IMF Conferences. While in London, he had fruitful talks with British Prime Minister Harold Wilson. He also had a stopover at Washington where he was able to convey India's views on the then existing Arab-Israeli conflict to the Vice President Herbert Humphrey and President Johnson. A TV interview took place while he was in Washington which was very well received and President Johnson himself congratulated Morarji on its success. Morarji visited the exhibition Expo-67 in Montreal during this visit. He also attended the Commonwealth Finance Ministers' Conference at Trinidad.

With a touchdown at Venezuela, Morarji arrived at Rio-de-Janeiro in Brazil to take part in the World Bank and IMF Conferences. He found Rio-de-Janeiro a beautiful city, located on the sea coast. He was deeply impressed by the famous statue of Jesus Christ, 'Christ the Redeemer', which had been put up on the summit of a hill that had to be reached by a ropeway. He found the city so located that the sea could be reached within 5 to 15 minutes from anywhere in the city. The World Bank Conference was the last one over which George Wood presided. He had good relations with Morarji having known him for quite a few years. Morarji was a highly respected figure in the IMF and World Bank circles, having held the Finance portfolio for a long time.

In March 1969, he represented India at President Dwight Eisenhower's funeral. He called on President Richard Nixon during this visit.

The year 1969 was to prove a major turning point not only in Morarji's life, but also in the history India. It was on the 3rd of May 1969 that India's much respected President Dr Zakir Hussain died. Mrs Gandhi was touring Rajasthan at this time and Morarji, as Deputy Prime Minister made arrangements for his body to be kept in state. It was this vacancy for the Presidency which let loose a chain of political events which no one could have possibly foreseen at that time. During his discussions with Mrs Gandhi, Morarji found her mentioning the name of Vice President V.V. Giri, for Presidency. Morarji was of the view that Giri had attracted a lot of criticism on account of his fondness for travel accompanied always by his family. Two other names being considered were that of Jagjivan Ram, the Union Agriculture Minister and D. Sanjivayya, former Chief Minister of Andhra Pradesh, as it was felt in a Gandhi Centenary year a candidate from the backward community, in deference to the Mahatma's ideals, should be elected to the post of President, the first citizen of India. Morarji felt that Jagjivan Ram, who was involved in a case of income-tax evasion, was not an appropriate choice (It was disclosed in Parliament that he had not paid his income tax for 10 years, though Jagjivan Ram claimed it was due to forgetfulness and not a deliberate misdemeanour). Sanjivayya was still too young though otherwise quite suitable. The name of Neelam Sanjeeva Reddy, the then Speaker of the Lok Sabha was also amongst one of the possible choices.

The discussions were not conclusive and various names were being floated around. Morarji returned from Germany in early July and flew straight to Bangalore from Bombay, where the AICC was to meet. The Congress candidate for Presidency was to be selected by the Parliamentary Board.

When Morarji arrived at Bangalore he found that Mrs Gandhi was yet to reach the session. Her arrival was delayed due to ill health, and she had sent a note with her 'stray thoughts' which included Bank Nationalisation, to be discussed at the AICC.

After some discussion, a compromise resolution moved by Morarji was approved unanimously by the AICC. However, much was to follow. On 12 July 1969 the Congress Parliamentary Board decided by a majority to support Sanjeeva Reddy over Jagjivan Ram as the Congress candidate for Presidency. To Mrs Gandhi's surprise, her Home Minister, Y.B. Chavan, had voted with the Syndicate for Sanjeeva Reddy. He had been assuring her of his support till the last moment. He was to do another volte-face on reaching Delhi and join Mrs Gandhi, in a day's time.

An attempt for a compromise was made between Mrs Gandhi and Congress President S. Nijalingappa, but it did not achieve much. On the Prime Minister's approval, Nijalingappa announced Sanjeeva Reddy's name on the 13th of July.

On 16 July 1969, at around 12:30 pm, Morarji received a letter from Indira Gandhi informing him that she was taking over the Finance Ministry. She asked him to continue as Deputy-Prime Minister and that the work to be assigned to him would be discussed later. Soon after this came an official announcement that the Prime Minister had taken charge of

Finance. Stung by a brazen attack on his self-respect, Morarji immediately resigned from the Cabinet. Being the No.2 man in the Cabinet and in the country, Morarji felt that the least courtesy of consulting him before changing his portfolio should have been adhered to by the Prime Minister, instead of the unilateral decision taken by her.

Mrs Gandhi, the next day, asked him to continue in the Cabinet as Deputy Prime Minister. Morarji made it clear that unless suitable amends were made, it would be impossible for him to do so. He could not and would not accept any office at the cost of his self-respect or honour. His resignation was accepted on 17 July, 1969 at around 4:00 pm. That very evening, the decision to nationalise 14 major banks was announced.

While making a statement in Parliament on his resignation, on 21 July 1969, Morarji said that during the period that he was Deputy Prime Minister, he had made a conscientious effort to perform his duties as Minister for Finance to pursue and implement the policies of the Party and the Cabinet from time to time. The Prime Minister, he added, in her letter relieving him of the charge of the Finance Ministry had cited his differences on certain basic issues of policy (Bank Nationalisation) and stated that she did not want to burden him with implementing these decisions. This despite the fact that he had moved the resolution himself on Bank Nationalisation at the AICC Session in Bangalore. He went on to state that he had only put on record the pros and cons of the issue while a discussion had taken place in the Working

Committee and this could not be construed as opposition; if it was otherwise he would not have moved the resolution in the AICC.

Turning to those in the Congress and opposition who considered him as opposed to progressive and socialist measures, Morarji went on to state that he had known poverty first hand in his youth and the eradication of poverty and upliftment of the masses had been one of his main guiding principles in public life. Quoting Gandhi's dictum that every interest which was in conflict with the interest of the down-trodden should be checked by governmental authority, he went on to add that he hoped the House would appreciate the correctness of his stand. In her reply Prime Minister Indira Gandhi was complimentary to Morarji's role as a freedom fighter and his strong sense of discipline. She tried to skirt the issue of asking for his resignation without verbally informing him, ultimately expressing regret that he had quit the Cabinet.

Soon thereafter, on the plea of 'Conscience Vote' the Prime Minister's supporters defeated the official Congress nominee Sanjeeva Reddy. V.V. Giri thus entered Rashtrapati Bhavan in August 1969. A split in the Congress became inevitable and it was in November 1969 that it was formalised with the expulsion of Mrs Gandhi by the Working Committee.

In the Opposition and in Detention (1970-1977)

Thus two groups of the Congress came into being. Mrs Gandhi's group known as the Congress (R) and the group of the other leaders known as the Congress (O) where (R) stood for Ruling and (O) for Organisation. The Congress (R) Government continued in office, even though it had been reduced to a minority on the floor of the Lok Sabha, as it had the support of the CPI and some other groups. However, in December 1970 the Lok Sabha was dissolved and mid-term polls called in March, 1971.

Morarji played a prominent part in these elections and the opposition formed a United Front, consisting of the Jan Sangh, Congress (O) and the Swatantra Party. However, as the unity was not strong enough, the ruling Congress got a thumping majority of 350 seats. The ruling party had much money and muscle power as well as the entire government machinery at its disposal. As events turned out, the euphoria having touched its peak with the Bangladesh War soon petered out.

By 1973, disenchantment was setting in with the Government's policies. Morarji as usual, was busy with campaigning for his party and playing an active role in Parliament.

The Nav Nirman Movement which started early in 1974 in Gujarat soon became a totally people's movement because of rising prices and allegations of corruption. The government of Chimanbhai Patel, which was then in power, used repression to crush it. The movement was centred on the issue of corruption and rising prices. Police atrocities mounted and Chimanbhai's government was dismissed by 9 February 1974. President's Rule was now imposed and the Assembly kept in suspended animation. As the government's repression continued, violence crept into the Nav Nirman Movement. Also the dissolution of the Assembly had to be secured, as it was the demand of the people.

Morarji decided that the time had come for him to enter the scene. On 9 March, 1974, he announced at Ahmedabad that he would undertake an indefinite fast to bring to an end the violence that had crept into the Nav Nirman Movement and to secure the just demand for the dissolution of the Gujarat Assembly. The Nav Nirman Movement has given ample proof that the Legislative Assembly had completely lost the confidence of the people.

Thus on 11 March 1974, Morarji began a fast unto death, at Ahmedabad. The fast had a large support from all sections of the people of Gujarat. By the 15th of March, the Government yielded to Morarji's rightful demand. The Gujarat Assembly was dissolved and it was announced the same evening.

A large crowd of people had gathered around the Gujarat Vidyapeeth Guest House where Morarji was staying. He at that time was talking to H.C. Sarin, a former Indian Civil Service Officer who was Advisor to the Governor of Gujarat during the duration of President's Rule.

As soon as Morarji went down the stairs of the Guest House to talk to the huge crowd of people gathered there, somebody shouted, 'We want Sarin.' This was because Sarin had publicly stated when he became the Advisor that he would crush the Nav Nirman Movement. Morarji immediately sensed that some violence may be resorted to by these people against Sarin, so, he stood holding on to the banisters of the staircase so that nobody could go up and manhandle Sarin, without hurting him first. (Sarin was on the first floor). Morarji could thus hold the crowd at bay till Sarin left through another entrance. This he could manage even though he was 78 years old at the time and had been fasting for four days. This was yet another instance of his admirable physical condition due to years of self discipline.

On 16th March, 1974, Morarji broke his fast accepting lime juice from the hands of Ravishankar Maharaj, a veteran Sarvodaya leader. The year 1974 was to prove crucial for India, for reasons more than one. As a very senior opposition leader, Morarji was very much in the hub of political events.

By the beginning of 1974, Jaya Prakash Narayan, a well known Sarvodaya leader, re-entered public life to fight against corruption and raise the cry for a cleaner public life. Students' Movements had already started in Gujarat and Bihar and thus Jaya Prakash or JP as he was fondly called, teamed up with the rest of the opposition to give impetus to it.

The movement spread all around northern India. Morarji was greeted by huge crowds wherever he went. In March 1974, the Congress had managed a majority in the UP Assembly elections by means which could hardly be termed fair. Rigging and similar unfair means were openly resorted to with total impunity. These events accelerated the pace of the opposition movement.

With the dawn of 1975, the situation was indeed getting more critical. Events now seemed to be moving fast. On 6 March 1975 People's March to Parliament took place, in which lakhs of people participated. A year had passed since the dissolution of the Gujarat Assembly in 1974. A very bad famine had hit Gujarat due to the failure of the 1974 monsoon. Morarji found, on his wide tours in these areas, that the relief provided was woefully inadequate. What was urgently required, he felt, was the need of a popular government and good governance.

It was in these circumstances he decided to stake his life once again. Morarji publicly announced that he would start a fast unto death on 7 April 1975, at his residence, 5 Dupleix Road, in Delhi. It was a fast aimed at the betterment of democracy in India. The basic demands of his fast were (i) Announcement of the Gujarat Assembly election date (ii) No use of 'MISA' (Maintenance of Internal Security Act) against political activists, and (iii) Repeal of external emergency which had come into force in the wake of the Bangladesh War. Before the fast, he had certain discussions with Prime Minister Indira Gandhi, at her request, which did not bring about any results.

The fast was a big success and a lot of people came to attend the prayer meetings in the evenings. The fast went on till 13th April 1975, when Mrs Gandhi sent Uma Shankar Dixit to inform Morarji that the Government was willing to meet his main demand, which was to announce the dates of the elections to the Gujarat Assembly. Regarding his other demands of repeal of MISA against political activists and the repeal of the External Emergency, the government gave assurances that these would also be met with at the earliest.

Since the Government had met his main demand of Assembly Elections in Gujarat, Morarji gave up his fast at the hands of Jaya Prakash Narayan at 5:30 pm on 13th April 1975. The Assembly Elections were due to be held in June 1975.

It was in these Assembly elections in Gujarat that opposition unity was to prove fruitful. The united opposition, which was named the Janata Morcha consisted of the Congress (O), Bharatiya Lok Dal, Jan Sangh and Socialist Party. Morarji spearheaded the campaign which was immensely successful. Despite being no match for the Congress in money and other resources, the Janata Morcha emerged victorious as the results of the Gujarat Assembly elections came in on 12 June, 1975. This heralded the formation of the Janata Morcha Government under Babubhai Patel.

On 12th June 1975, an epoch-making event took place which was to change drastically the political destiny of the subcontinent. It was on this day that the Allahabad High Court unseated Prime Minister Indira Gandhi from the Lok Sabha on the basis of an election petition filed by her opponent at Rae Bareli, Raj Narain. In the days that went by immediately after the Allahabad Judgment, it became clear that Mrs Gandhi did not want to resign as per the established norm or convention. The Congress went on expressing faith in her leadership and holding solidarity rallies to this effect. The opposition naturally went on the offensive. A Lok Sangarsh Samiti, with Morarji as

Chairman, was formed and it chalked out a programme of action which was to start with a mass satyagraha on 29 June to force the Prime Minister to resign.

On 25 June 1975 the opposition held a huge public meeting at the Ramlila Grounds at Delhi. Morarji, JP and various other opposition leaders were present. JP gave an appeal to the army and police not to obey illegal orders. Although Morarji and the others did not know it then, they were to receive a proverbial midnight knock on their doors.

It was early in the morning of 26 June 1975, that the police came in search of Morarji to arrest him under the Maintenance of Internal Security Act (MISA). It was indeed an unkind cut that Morarji was being arrested by the very Government of which he was once the Deputy Prime Minister.

As is well known all the major opposition leaders were rounded up. Morarji took his arrest stoically. He felt that it was the will of God. Immediately after his arrest he was taken to the Sohna Tourist Centre Guest House in Gurgaon District, Haryana.

It was here and later at Taoru in the same District that he would spend the next one-and-a-half years of his life. Jaya Prakash Narayan was also kept in Sohna, in an adjacent suite, but he and Morarji were not allowed to meet. Later JP was moved to Chandigarh. On the day of his arrest, Morarji decided that he would not take cooked food any longer. Since then he lived on milk and fruit. He felt that his life in detention was a boon, a blessing in disguise, as he could concentrate wholly and solely on God. During the first month he was not allowed to go out during the day and therefore he refused to go out in the night for a walk.

He walked inside his room which he did not leave for the first one month of detention. He told the police that he was not a thief to be allowed only to walk in the night. Only after one month was he given permission to walk in the mornings. After some days he found that his door was locked from the outside. He told the officer in charge of the security that if they continued to lock it from the outside he would do so from the inside. The level of high handedness the then government showed to political prisoners was atrocious, totally beyond comprehension or belief. The fact that the officials in the Sohna Guest House knew that Morarji was to be brought there on the morning of the 26th June, the previous evening showed that the Declaration of the Emergency had been planned earlier and was not the result of JP's speech at the Ramlila Maidan as claimed by Mrs Indira Gandhi. This was also reaffirmed and corroborated later by other evidence unearthed during the Shah Commission of Inquiry.

Morarji was a person who could attune himself to any situation. In addition to prayer, reciting and reading his beloved Gita, he updated his autobiography and wrote a small book on 'Nature Cure.' He did his spinning, yoga and other daily chores. Later, when the police allowed it, he began walking up to the road, outside his place of detention. The police officers could not keep pace with him, even though Morarji was 80 years old. The police officer would sit while he walked.

Morarji did not challenge his detention in court as he had never believed in doing this, even when he courted arrest during the freedom struggle. His daughter-in-law, Mrs Padma Desai, had gone to court on her own accord on his right to interviews.

Morarji followed the rules of the prison scrupulously during his period of detention. As per the rules only people listed for appointments could meet him. Once a close acquaintance of his managed to enter his room by somehow dodging the guards. Morarji said that he could only greet him but the person should sit outside without meeting him as his name did not figure in the list of persons to be given an interview. He did not believe in breaking rules no matter what his differences with the government may have been

Despite being in detention, Morarji could realise that the country was reeling under the oppression of a dictatorial regime. Having full confidence in this nation's citizens, he knew that they would and could liberate themselves, sooner or later. As it turned out, the opportunity presented itself sooner than later. He always believed that adversity is a major contributor in building one's character in life. 'Unless you pass through difficulties you can never learn a lesson. This is the lesson I have learnt in life. It is only the hard way which leads you to fulfilment of life. No virtue can be obtained easily. You have to pass through the test – otherwise there is no virtue.' (Interview to *India Today*, 31 Aug 1979)

Morarji spent the rest of 1975, and the whole of 1976, in detention following the above mentioned routine. Then came the year of destiny, 1977.

The First Non-Congress Prime Minister (1977)

On 18 January, 1977, as was his habit, Morarji had risen early. He went about his daily routine. That afternoon a few police officers entered his room. They told him he was being released unconditionally. Since Morarji had no money on him, he said that the local administration would have to arrange for a vehicle to take him to his Delhi residence. The Deputy Commissioner of Gurgaon was contacted and a car arranged. He reached Delhi by the evening. By then most other major political personalities of the opposition groups had been released from detention. Mrs Gandhi had dissolved the Lok Sabha and elections were to be held in March. Immediately, therefore, Morarji and other opposition leaders decided that the time was ripe for the formation of a United opposition party.

After a round of hectic negotiations, on 20 January 1977, the formation of the Janata Party was announced at Morarji's residence, 5 Dupleix Road. It consisted of the Congress (O), Bharatiya Lok Dal (BLD), Jan Sangh and the Socialist Party. Morarji Desai was named the Chairman of the party and Chaudhary Charan Singh, Deputy Chairman. On 30 January

1977 Morarji launched the campaign for the opposition along with Atal Bihari Vajpayee at a massive rally at the Ramlila Grounds, Delhi. On the same date Charan Singh inaugurated the campaign at Kanpur and Jaya Prakash Narayan at Patna. The response to the campaign from the public was overwhelming for the Janata Party. Despite the lack of funds and machinery the rallies drew huge crowds, Morarji was spearheading the campaign as Chairman of the new party.

On 2 February, 1977, Mrs Gandhi's Minister for Agriculture and Food, Jagjivan Ram, quit the Congress along with the former Chief Ministers of Uttar Pradesh and Orissa (now Odisha) H.N. Bahuguna and Nandini Satpathy respectively. This group also aligned themselves with the Janata Party.

The hectic campaigning which took place in the spring of 1977 will remain etched in the memories of those who witnessed it. By end February despite all its resources the Congress was in poor shape in northern India. By then the whole nation was of the view that Morarji would have to lead the country now. There was no doubt that he was the most experienced and senior leader available at that juncture.

It was a historic campaign with the people determined to liberate themselves from a dictatorial apparatus; the family planning excesses, the most unpopular move, playing heavily on the peoples' mind.

The results began coming in on 20th March and by midnight they were fully known. The people of northern India rejected the Congress, lock, stock and barrel. The Janata-CFD Combine notched up an impressive tally of 300 seats. All over northern

India people celebrated with great euphoria. There had not been celebrations on such a vast scale since 1947.

On 23 March, Jaya Prakash Narayan arrived in Delhi for the naming of the Janata Prime Minister. Developments in Delhi moved fast, and it had become known that the Jan Sangh group was now supporting Jagjivan Ram in the race for Prime Ministership. However it was known that J.P. Narayan as well as J.B. Kripalani were in favour of Morarji's name. Other groupings within the Janata Party including the BLD and the Congress (O) supported Morarji. This was natural as he was the seniormost and the most experienced leader and administrator on the scene who had also been in detention and solitary confinement for nineteen months during the Emergency.

Jagjivan Ram, on the other hand, had been in the Union Cabinet throughout the Emergency and was, in fact, the person who had moved the Emergency resolution in Parliament. On the evening of 23rd March after the crowds had cleared from the grounds of the Gandhi Peace Foundation, where Jaya Prakash Narayan was staying, four Sarvodaya men, Radhakrishnan, Secretary Gandhi Peace Foundation (GPF), Sidharaj Dhadda, Narayan Desai, and Govind Rao Deshpande got into action with the help of some aides and supporters of Morarji.

They were active throughout the night of 23-24 March and were able to convey to the Jan Sangh group the support of Jaya Prakash Narayan to Morarji Desai, whereupon the Jan Sangh agreed to go along with Jaya Prakash Narayan's wishes. On the morning of 24th March, 1977, Morarji, in the presence of

Jaya Prakash Narayan and Kripalaniji, took an oath to fulfil the unfinished tasks of the father of the nation at Rajghat.

On the forenoon of the same day the Janata Party Deputy Chairman and BLD leader Chaudhary Charan Singh wrote a letter to JP conveying his support for Morarji. At 12:20 pm Morarji, dressed in his usual white khadi attire, entered the Central Hall of Parliament (the venue of the Janata Parliamentary Party meeting). One wonders if memories of 19 January 1966, when he was defeated in the contest for the Prime Ministership by Indira Gandhi in this very hall entered his mind; stoic as always I doubt if he would have devoted much thought to it. But today was a day of victory, it was but appropriate that it should be in the very same hall where his political career had reached its nadir and many a scribe had written him off as a has-been in the country's public life. Such are the turns of the wheel of destiny. At the meeting of Janata Parliamentary Party for the election of the leader, Jagjivan Ram was also present, but later left the meeting in a huff once he came to know that Morarji was to be unanimously elected by the Janata Parliamentary Party. However, later a compromise solution was worked out under which Jagjivan Ram joined the new Cabinet.

As JP announced Morarji's name a thunderous applause reverberated through the Central Hall of Parliament. It represented the glorious spirit of 1977. Morarji's acceptance speech was full of humility and dignity in which he thanked the people's representatives for the trust they had reposed in him. Jaya Prakash Narayan in his remarks said that people's power and state power should work hand-in-hand. On which Morarji made an assertion to the effect that he would act accordingly. On hearing this JP became emotional and said that even though younger to Desai in age, he would leave the world earlier, but he would go with this great assurance. As this exchange took place the Central Hall reverberated with cheers, and many of the Members of Parliament had tears in their eyes. An epoch making event had just happened. As per the established procedure two Janata Party Members of Parliament, Raj Narain and George Fernandes as well as the General Secretary L.K. Advani called on the Acting President Jatti to inform him of Morarji's election. Soon after, the Acting President invited Morarji to be the next Prime Minister of India. Before taking office, Morarji called on the outgoing Prime Minister Indira Gandhi.

At 3:30 pm on Thursday, 24 March 1977, Morarji was sworn in as the Prime Minister of India. The Ashoka Hall of Rashtrapati Bhavan was packed to capacity. As he intoned the oath of office and secrecy, it was as if a new dawn was heralded in the history of the Indian subcontinent. His first engagement as Prime Minister was a press conference; this monthly date with the media he religiously kept during his Prime Ministership; apart from Jawaharlal Nehru no other Prime Minister had been as interactive with the fourth estate as Morarji was. The Vigyan Bhavan was a scene of bonhomie that day, no questions were banned, no answers held back. Some of the highlights were, to strive to end poverty and unemployment, to undo the damage of the 42nd Amendment and bring about improvement in governance. He also said he did not believe in a committed bureaucracy and felt that everyone should do his duty. In reply to one of the questions he denied that it was his ambition to become Prime Minister, stating, 'the ambition of my life is to realise truth and God, never has it been the Prime Ministership of the nation.' Some wisecracks also featured as the journalists were apprehensive of whether a man at 81 would be able to do justice to the Prime Ministerial responsibilities. Pat came the reply, 'According to the English calendar I am only 18.' (He was born in a leap year). He also mentioned that he did not have the technology to undo a vasectomy in the context of the Family Planning excesses during the emergency.

The same evening he addressed a huge rally at the Ramlila Ground, where barely two months ago he had launched the opposition campaign. He told the people that his government should not be feared as they were the people's servants, not masters. He told them to 'box his ears' if he went wrong. Some fears had been removed but some remained, it would be the duty of the government to eliminate these. Morarji also appealed to the people not to hesitate to point out the mistakes of the new government peacefully, while cautioning that the peace of the graveyard was neither welcome nor acceptable.

On the next day, the cabinet took office. Morarji selected his team with ability. His prominent Ministers were Charan Singh Home Affairs, A.B. Vajpayee External Affairs, H.M. Patel Finance, Madhu Dandavate Railways, Biju Patnaik Steel and Mines, Prakash Singh Badal Food and Agriculture, and L.K. Advani Information & Broadcasting. On the 28th of March, 1977, the Cabinet was expanded to include Jagjivan Ram as Defence Minister, (he had held the portfolio during the

Bangladesh War), H.N. Bahuguna Petroleum, George Fernandes who was first given Communications and then Industry, and Raj Narain Health and Family Welfare. Raj Narain had defeated Mrs Gandhi at Rae Bareli.

Altogether, it was one of the most talented Cabinets in post-Independence India. On the 4th of April 1977, Morarji delivered his inaugural address to the nation on radio and TV. He told the nation that evening that he was addressing the people of India as a humble custodian of their trust. He reminded them that their faith in the battle against Money Power had brought about the Janata Government which was an instrument of their faith. He asserted that self-discipline, and not Emergency, was the need of the hour for India.

He made it clearly known that his government would look after the interests of the whole of India not only the northern part. He said he was aware of the fact that for the first time since Independence the opposition was on trial as the ruling party; his government would give priority to economic stability and novel programmes like Antodaya. The Anti-Defection law was to be given top-priority.

While speaking on the motion of thanks to the President's Address on 5 April 1977, Morarji made a general statement on the policies of his government both domestic and international, underlying his philosophy of governance, making it clear that India got freedom very easily from the British, he said that the price of freedom had to be paid during the 20 months of the Emergency and hoped that no other price would have to be paid for freedom. At any rate he added the opposition would not have to pay any price. He said that his party wanted the country to be great, happy, strong and help human society become happy. This would be the common aim of the opposition and the government. However, Morarji recalled that Mahatma Gandhi had said that whatever your aims and however laudable they maybe these cannot be achieved unless the means were pure. If anything had plagued India for long years he reminded his fellow parliamentarians it was fear, and unless that feeling of fear was removed all efforts of development would not succeed and in this common endeavour he asked for the co-operation of the members of all parties both of the government and the opposition. There would be no true democracy unless fear was removed from our land. The speech underlined Morarji's philosophy of life and his thinking for future governments of India as well. No government, however mighty, may continue for long if it created a fear psychosis among the people, he cautioned.

A controversy surrounded his interview with *Time* Magazine during which he said that he had changed his opinion about women in politics after his experience with three women Prime Ministers: Golda Meir, Indira Gandhi and Srimavo Bandaranaike. Because, he said women on the whole have better softer qualities than men, and on the whole they don't go as devilish as men. But when a woman becomes devilish, she beats all records and no man can equal her. This led to a furore as women's groups demonstrated in front of his residence and he had to clarify that he did not mean any offence to Indian women. Another storm in a teacup!

In the same interview he made his views about atomic weapons very clear and said that India would never produce Atomic Weapons which he felt was among the greatest enemies of mankind and he would strive to see that nuclear weapons disappeared from the surface of the world. However idealistic this may seem it gives expression to the man's inner philosophy. It is certain that he would have vehemently opposed the decision of the Vajpayee government to test in a nuclear device at Pokhran in 1998 had he been alive. In this conversation with *Time*, he mentioned that he held the view that it was the most important function of the government to make people fearless as they are more afraid of the government than any other agency, which in turn should see to it that no honest man would be made to suffer under the government. Then, he said, one could create more honest men.

Morarji was fairly articulate when giving expression to his views on the state of affairs of the nation which he inherited as Prime Minister which he described as 'widespread corruption, unemployment, unprecedented rise in prices, lowest value of rupee and highest disparities of income with 70% of our people living below the subsistence level.' (Letter to former Lok Sabha Speaker Anantasayanam Ayyangar on 22 July, 1977).

During the weeks that followed, Morarji set about getting the government moving in various respects. Particularly on the economic front his government was to record impressive achievements. New schemes like 'Food for Work' and 'Antodaya' were conceived. In the coming months, his government was to remove all restrictions on the movement of foodgrains and other essential commodities. The price rise was firmly halted and essential commodities were freely available everywhere. Sugar and cooking oil were to sell at ₹2.35 and ₹7/- a kilo respectively during the coming two years.

The eminent advocate Nani A. Palkhivala, (later appointed Ambassador to the USA by the Janata Government) addressing Morarji on his election and describing the end of the Emergency wrote, 'The gruesome nightmare is over. It is your great destiny to lead the nation after its second liberation to the broad sunny uplands. The people – one sixth of the human race – have given you a generous and confident mandate. Only one man in a billion is born with your destiny.' (N.A. Palkhivala: "An Open Letter to the Prime Minister" *The Illustrated Weekly of India*, 17 April 1977).

On 30 April 1977 the Janata Government under Article 356 of the Constitution ordered fresh assembly elections in states of northern India where the Congress had been routed in the March poll. In June 1977, the Janata Party swept to power in these states. This move of the Janata Government has been criticised by constitutional pundits and journalists as an infringement of the federal structure of the constitution. However, one thing has to be borne in mind while discussing the issue. Except Uttar Pradesh and Orissa (now Odisha) all the other assemblies had completed their five year tenure having been elected in 1972. These Assemblies were continuing to exist on the new six-year term given to them by the 42nd Amendment which the Janata Party was committed to repeal. Therefore the dismissal of the Uttar Pradesh and Orissa Assemblies can only be considered arbitrary if one considers this aspect. However, it can be said in the defence of the dissolution of these two State assemblies that sometimes political reasons lead to otherwise illogical decisions. The Congress (I) returned the compliment in 1980 on its assumption of power when it dismissed all the Janata Party State Governments. It is to Morarji's credit that he allowed a totally free and fair poll in Jammu & Kashmir in June 1977, which heralded the return of Sheikh Abdullah to power. This was the first time a poll in Jammu & Kashmir was so free and fair. A great believer in decentralisation, Morarji saw to it, during his Premiership, that states were fully allowed to use their federal powers. Too much central authority, except in matters of national interest, would hamper the all around development of the states, he felt.

With regard to the various Commissions of Inquiry going into the Emergency excesses Morarji felt that the government should not take any vindictive action, whatsoever. During his first few months in office, Morarji toured various parts of the country.

One of the issues the Janata Government had to face within a few months of assuming office was the election of the President as the incumbent President Fakhruddin Ali Ahmed had passed away in February 1977. B.D. Jatti, the Vice President, was acting as President. Neelam Sanjeeva Reddy, the Congress candidate of 1969 had been elected as Speaker of the Lok Sabha in March 1977 and was a candidate this time around as well. However, Morarji was in favour of a non-political person, preferably a woman, for the office of President. He suggested the name of Rukmini Devi Arundale who had done commendable work in setting up the Kalakshetra Academy of Dance and Music as well as playing a stellar role in the field of Animal Welfare, being instrumental in getting passed the Prevention of Cruelty to Animals Act, and being the first Chairperson of the Animal Welfare Board. Even Indira Gandhi had expressed support to Mrs Arundale's candidature and the leader of the opposition Yashwantrao Chavan had concurred with this proposal. However, within the ruling Janata Party Sanjeeva Reddy's name was finding more support, particularly among the Socialist group and the Charan Singh led BLD. Seeing his colleagues in a majority, Morarji went along with Reddy's name, a decision he would later regret. It must be said to his credit that he ensured an unanimous election for the President's office, an event which had never happened before and has never happened after either.

Morarji once said that Democracy originated in India and is very much part of the Indian psyche. This helps explain the opposition victory in 1977 as well as the changes in many mighty governments in our country over the years that followed. He said that evidence for this was to be found in the Vedas which described democratically elected republics in our country much before the establishment of the democracy in Ancient Greece. Many historians including Professor Steve Muhlberger of the Nipissing University of Canada have given evidence of establishment of democracy in the Vedic period. Once when it was pointed out to Morarji that the British feel democracy was the gift of the English administration to India, he said that he had no quarrel on that score, 'if it pleased their vanity!'

It has become fashionable in some quarters to give the view publicity that Morarji and some of his contemporaries who were in the Janata Government of 1977 were anti Jawaharlal Nehru ideologically and politically. Fortunately Morarji's views on Nehru and his philosophy are recorded for posterity. He is on record to have said, 'Nehru was a true democrat and a worthy inheritor of Gandhi's mantle. He had his weaknesses of course. Like his desire for dynastic succession. But he was a good leader, a patriot. He understood India.' (Interview by Pritish Nandy, *The Illustrated Weekly of India*, 2 February, 1986).

The Janata Government also took steps to free the electronic media from government control. The appointment of the committee headed by well-known journalist B.G. Verghese early in its tenure was a step in this direction. The committee submitted its report in March 1978. In a letter to L.K. Advani, Minister for Information and Broadcasting, on 15 March 1978, Morarji felt that the intention of the government was to provide greater freedom for the electronic media and greater scope within the media for able professionals imbued with a spirit of public service.

Sometime towards the end of September 1977, Morarji Desai, under pressure from his cabinet colleagues like Atal Bihari Vajpayee, George Fernandes and L.K. Advani who were pressing the cabinet to bring Indira Gandhi to book for the Emergency excesses gave Home Minister Charan Singh the go-ahead to arrest Indira Gandhi. He gave Charan Singh a few clear instructions that she should not be ill-treated on any account, the case should be fool-proof against her and she should be offered bail. Charan Singh erred while executing the arrest by the CBI, as he did not consult the Law Minister or the Attorney-General on the issue and relied totally on IPS officers. The case against Mrs Gandhi included misuse of power in the following: an agreement with a French firm Campagnie Francaise De Petroles for off-shore drilling by the ONGC near Mumbai, allegedly causing a loss of ₹11 crores to the exchequer, large-scale donations forcibly from textile manufacturers and illegal supply of 100 Jeeps for the elections to the Congress Party. The Magistrate ordered Mrs Gandhi's release the very next day as the prosecution was unable to provide the source of the accusations causing immense embarrassment to the Janata Government; in fact it put her back on the comeback trail. The CBI had bungled things up badly.

Combating social evils for the betterment of society as he believed in, Morarji took up the implementation of Prohibition on a nationwide basis, since he felt that 90 per cent of the people who drank liquor in India were the poverty-stricken masses who could ill afford liquor. It assumed paramount importance. Education was another subject close to Morarji's heart. At least 30 per cent of government expenditure should be in the field of education, he is once reported to have said.

In August 1977, the Israeli Foreign Minister General Moshe Dayan paid a secret visit to India. In his meeting with Morarji he tried to persuade India to allow Israeli planes to refuel in India for a proposed strike on the Pakistani nuclear facility at Kahuta but got a firm no from the Indian Prime Minister. Morarji also made it amply clear to Dayan that Israel would have to vacate the Golan Heights and other occupied Arab territories before it could move for furthering relations with India. The visit was kept secret, probably because of an expected adverse fallout from countries of the Muslim world, but later when the Congress Government in 1980 revealed the fact, Morarji gave a statement accepting the fact that he did meet Dayan. In this context later Morarji said, 'I did not allow people to know that he came because he wanted to keep it a secret. But when someone asked me I admitted it. I also explained why I had done it. I did not lie. In fact, even when I met him, I did not do it alone, secretly. I kept the Foreign Minister present at the time. We did not invite him. He wanted to come on his own. We agreed only to listen to him.' (Interview with Pritish Nandy, *The Illustrated Weekly of India*, 2 February, 1986).

Charting a New Course in the Indian Subcontinent (1977-78)

Morarji left on his first foreign tour as Prime Minister, on 21 October, 1977 on a visit to the Soviet Union. At Moscow Airport, he was greeted by President Brezhnev, who had broken protocol to come to receive Morarji. 'Welcome to Moscow' he greeted, as Morarji walked briskly out of the Air India aircraft. 'The weather is sunny, though cold' remarked Foreign Minister Andrei Gromyko, as he greeted him. It had been raining for the last few days and the sun had just come out that day.

After driving with him from the airport, Morarji had a round of talks with President Brezhnev that day itself. The meeting took place in the Kremlin, inside Katherine Hall that was adorned with beautiful chandeliers. During his speech at a banquet hosted by President Brezhnev, Morarji spoke of the 'Revolution of the Ballot Box,' in March 1977 in which he said two hundred million men and women were the heroes. 1977 happened to be the Diamond Jubilee of the 'October Revolution' of the USSR. Morarji also stressed on continued Indo-Soviet co-operation.

On 22nd October, Morarji visited the Black Sea Holiday Resort of Sochi. Here he saw the famous Matsesta Springs. He was awarded, what was called 'Diploma with a Smile' from the

Matsesta Sanatorium. Morarji said this was in tune with his philosophy of life. On the 23rd he visited Ukraine and Kiev. Morarji and his entourage witnessed the Ukrainian Ballet *The Forest* based on the fairy tale by that name.

On the 25th of October, Morarji returned to Moscow where he spoke to the people over Soviet Television. He spoke of the need to remove fear from the minds of the people the world over. He also mentioned the personal equation he had developed with Soviet leaders and expressed the hope that renewed ties would develop between both the countries.

Morarji went around and saw the development plans of the city for the year 2000. He and President Brezhnev signed a joint declaration on the 26 October, 1977 wherein the Soviets gave a commitment for more aid to India. On the same day Morarji was awarded a PhD from Moscow State University. Morarji returned home on 27th October. His first foreign trip as Prime Minister was the beginning of the extremely successful foreign policy his government perused during the coming two years.

All through his life, Morarji had exhibited exemplary courage in all his dealings, which he claimed stems from his unshakeable faith in God. On 11 October, 1977, while going to Surat from Bombay by the Frontier Mail, he ignored a bomb scare that had arisen due to anonymous telephone calls. He brushed aside the pleadings of his security staff that he should go by air and went by the same train.

'Life without adventure is meaningless,' Morarji had said on 28 October, 1977, while talking to Sir Edmund Hillary and members of the 'Ocean to Sky' Expedition. Two days later, he was to be part of an adventure.

On 30th October, while watching naval exercises on board the INS Dunagiri, along with top Naval Brass and Defence Minister Jagjivan Ram, Morarji saw Jack-staying in operation. Jack-staying is when a chair tied to a rope is passed between two ships in motion on the high seas, enabling a person to move from one ship to another. That day in Bombay, after the Naval Chief Jal Cursetji explained how safe jack-staying was and went on it himself, Morarji said he would follow suit. Defence Minister Jagjivan Ram and Air Chief Marshal Moolgavkar, who was also present, tried to dissuade him, but he went ahead on the jack-stay from *INS Dunagiri* to *INS Nilgiri* and back. A man jack-staying at 81 years of age was certainly a record. He gave anxious moments to the others present, but said he liked the experience. To journalists present, Morarji said, 'I am never frightened of these things.'

On the 4 November 1977, Prime Minister Morarji Desai and his entourage left Calcutta for Jorhat, en route to the north-eastern states. Arunachal Pradesh was on the itinerary. He flew in an Indian Air Force TU-124. On board with him were Narayan Desai, a Sarvodaya leader, Arunachal Chief Minister Prem Thungon, his son Kantibhai and other officials and members of his staff. The weather over Jorhat had been somewhat unclear since that afternoon, but not abnormal for night landing. Alternative landing arrangements at the Air Force Station at Chhabua and Tezpur had been made, in case the Prime Minister's plane had to be diverted from Jorhat.

However, the pilot did not divert and proceeded to Jorhat. At around 7:40 pm, passengers were asked to fasten their seat belts. According to John Lobo, Chief Security Liaison Officer to the Prime Minister at that time, the plane made a low pass near the tarmac of the airfield. However the pilot could not land and commenced another landing circuit pulling up the aircraft. Lobo tried to gain access to the cockpit so as to ascertain from the Captain if he had plans to divert and change course due to climatic reasons. Lobo could not do so as the door handle seemed stuck and was not opening. Morarji, witnessing Lobo's action, asked Lobo to return to his seat. The plane dipped, rose again and then crashed into a marshy field. Once the crash had occurred the passengers gathered their wits and called out to each other, the main concern of the staff being to ask if Morarji was all right as the lights of the aircraft had gone off. Morarji said he was okay and formed a chain with the rest of the passengers and evacuated through the rear of the plane. He simply slid down the panel on a water logged paddy field where the aircraft had landed. It later transpired that when the aeroplane was cruising at a speed of 300 mph it cut through a clump of tall trees, a mishap which should not have occurred. It was obvious there had been a mechanical failure of some kind.

Due to the impact, all the crew died. There was no fire though the under-carriage of the belly had been damaged. Morarji was unhurt except for minor injuries and cuts on the lip. He kept his calm remaining unperturbed throughout the crisis. The villagers of Tekla Gaon, where the crash occurred, rendered assistance. Morarji walked for three kilometres through the fields to the airport. Some members of Morarji's entourage suffered injuries. His son Kantibhai suffered a compound fracture on the leg.

As soon as the aircraft's lights went out, Air Force search parties in helicopters went out looking for the Prime Minister's plane. On the evening of Morarji's crash, the Chief of the Air Staff, Air Chief Marshal Moolgavkar was at a diplomatic party in honour of Sir Malcolm MacDonald. It was here at 8:20 pm, that he received the chilling news that the Prime Minister's plane had lost contact with the Air Traffic Control. However, soon after, it became known that Morarji was safe. Soon after arrival at Jorhat, the injured were taken to the Military Hospital.

The next morning an MI-8 Helicopter ferried Morarji to Tezpur, with his entourage. From Tezpur Air Chief Marshal Moolgavkar flew him back to Delhi in another TU-124, 'Rajhans'. Morarji was none the worse despite the scary accident and looked as fresh as a daisy, when he alighted. President Sanjeeva Reddy, Vice President B.D. Jatti and many other leaders greeted him and wished him a long life.

The TU-124, in which Morarji crashed was a Russian aircraft of 1965 vintage. Air Chief Marshal Moolgavkar also expressed his gratitude to God that the Prime Minister had escaped unhurt at the accident.

On alighting at Delhi, when a pressman asked Morarji if he would not like to skip office and take rest in view of the trauma of the crash, Morarji said, 'Nothing doing'. In a broadcast on the evening of 5th November, Morarji thanked God for saving him. He wanted to rededicate himself to the service of the nation. Describing the Indian Air Force as very efficient, he paid rich tributes to the officers who had died in the crash and mentioned that he had asked the Air Chief to see to it that their families got adequate compensation. He thanked the people for the affection shown to him.

The Jorhat crash was another instance of the major role that providence plays in men's lives.

In 1977 Morarji made a statement in a press interview that he had for a considerable period of time been consuming some ounces of his own urine every morning. This caused considerable bewilderment among the Indian public and led to some jibes in the media also. In the following year, 1978, he published a booklet titled *Nature Cure* in which he gave a comprehensive description of the practice and its benefits. Some others including former Naval Chief Admiral Ramdas have adopted the practice of Auto Urine Therapy. Many people felt that as usual Morarji showed exemplary courage by talking about an exercise he was indulging in without caring about mass public reaction or criticism to something unconventional. However a good number of people also felt he should have kept this under wraps while holding such a high and esteemed office. It was bound to create loose talk and bring ridicule to the office of Prime Minister of the world's largest democracy. Well, it is up to the readers to form their own personal opinion on the topic.

In the time given to him as Prime Minister, from 1977 onwards, Morarji saw to it that the rural masses of the country got a fair deal. It was during his tenure that rural development was given a big boost and the allocation of funds for rural development was highly increased. When he took over, there were 1,20,000 villages in the country which did not have drinking water facilities. Over the next two years 50,000 of these villages were provided with drinking water.

In 1977 itself, Morarji announced the setting up of 'Minorities Commission' for the first time since Independence. It was formed early in 1978, under the Chairmanship of Minoo Masani. By the time 1978 dawned Morarji was well into making new forays in various fields. On 1 January, 1978, President Jimmy Carter visited India with his wife Rosalyn. The visit was a remarkable success. Carter was able to hit it off well with Prime Minister Desai and they had fruitful talks. Carter and his wife were able to visit places of interest in Delhi, also a civic reception was organised in Delhi which was largely attended by the people of Delhi. President Carter with Mrs Carter also visited a Haryana village during the India trip. Prime Minister Morarji Desai accompanied him to the village, where they were received by the Haryana Chief Minister Devi Lal. President Carter saw a typical Indian village.

During his cordial talks with President Carter, the question of Nuclear Non-Proliferation Treaty (NPT) came up and Morarji naturally took a strong stand on the issue, as it was in India's interest. It was after this meeting that, it was leaked to the press by mistake, Carter had told one of his aides that the Indian Government would get something cold and stiff from his administration on his return. Morarji heard about the leak and in his next meeting told Carter with his characteristic bluntness, 'Why wait till you get back to be *cold and stiff*? Why not start it right now?' Carter could appreciate Morarji's open and candid nature and his forthrightness and thereafter developed a very warm relationship with him.

At the end of the visit, Carter and Morarji signed a joint 'Declaration' pledging renewed efforts for 'Global Peace' and Indo-US Co-operation in various fields.

The early months of 1978 saw renewed political activity with the Congress splitting into two groups and Assembly elections in Andhra, Maharashtra, Assam and Karnataka scheduled to take place. Morarji campaigned extensively during these elections which saw the Janata Party come to power in Assam and emerge as a force to reckon with in Maharashtra. However, by March-April 1978, certain fissures had begun to develop in the Janata Government. Charan Singh, the Home Minister, had begun efforts to achieve his 'Life's ambition' to become the Prime Minister.

Of course, it would be incorrect to blame Charan Singh alone. There were many others in the Janata Government who wanted the Prime Ministership. In March 1978 Morarji went on TV and radio to address the people on the completion of one year of Janata rule. He had many reasons to be justifiably proud. His Government had firmly halted inflationary trends, maintained a good law and order situation and done extremely well on foreign policy.

By April-May 1978, the BLD Group mounted an offensive against the Party President Chandra Shekhar, with the aim of capturing the Party organisation as soon as possible. In May 1978, Charan Singh suffered a heart-attack and after a stay at the All India Institute of Medical Sciences, where Morarji visited him, he left for Suraj Kund on the Haryana-Delhi border to recuperate. It was to be the setting of another political battle in the offing. The offensive against Chandra Shekhar continued to mount, with Health Minister Raj Narain leading the attack. Many prominent leaders of the Janata Party shuttled between Delhi and Suraj Kund to hammer out a solution but this was not of much avail. Raj Narain had begun to mount an attack on the Jan Sangh group of the Janata also.

Morarji was waiting and watching the whole scene. He was hopeful that an amicable solution could be reached. On 5 June, 1978, he left on an extensive foreign tour, a tour which would win India many friends, with stopovers at Brussels, Tehran and a two day visit to London. Morarji arrived in New York to address the United Nations General Assembly on 9 June, 1978.

He appealed to the member countries of the United Nations that the time had come to outlaw Military Nuclear Weapons. Morarji felt that a total freeze should be brought about on the future development of Nuclear Arms. He felt that an independent inspection for safeguards should take place.

In a speech listened to with rapt attention, he went on, 'Life and death are poised on a razor's edge. Let us choose life. There is a moral imperative to work for the abolition of war.' The press was to comment the next day that the language used by Mr Desai that had extensive quotations from the scriptures was of a kind that was rarely heard in the halls of the United Nations. As he finished, a thunderous applause awaited him. All through the world, India's image soared sky-high.

On 13 June, 1978 Morarji and his entourage arrived at the Andrews Air Force Base, near Washington. He was received by Secretary of State Cyrus Vance and later President Carter accorded him a reception on the White House Lawns. In his welcome speech, he described Mr Desai as 'a man of great courage and principles from a great country.' Morarji added an informal touch to the reception by going around and greeting people present on the White House Lawns. That evening President Carter hosted a banquet in his honour.

During the visit, Morarji came out very well with the American Press. An American mother from California appealed to the Prime Minister, when he was in America, to help find her lost daughter who was hooked on to the 'Sadhu Syndrome' in India. She wrote to him C/o the White House and received a sympathetic reply. Earlier, during his tour of Australia, a father, whose son was missing in the Bay of Bengal, appealed to Prime Minister Desai for help at the Andaman Islands. On Morarji's intervention, he received the help which had earlier been turned down by the concerned authorities. Morarji, as always, looked at things from the human angle.

On 17 June, 1978, Morarji landed at Delhi. The political situation was on the boil. The Charan Singh group had accelerated their campaign. At the airport itself, Morarji roundly ticked off Raj Narain, when the latter spread 'attar' (perfume) on him. 'During my absence you have been spreading all kinds of foul smell and now you apply perfume on me,' he told the Health Minister. It was an indication that he would deal with things firmly. At the airport press conference, Morarji made it clear that there was no need for Chandra Shekhar to quit the Party Presidentship (one of the main demands of the Charan Singh-Raj Narain group).

On the 25th of June, at a public meeting in Kota he declared that his Health Minister, Raj Narain, could leave the Cabinet if he did not mend his ways. Morarji issued an open warning that indiscipline would not be tolerated any longer.

On the 29th of June, Charan Singh went to the press in a statement issued at Suraj Kund (where he was convalescing after his recent illness). He expressed his displeasure at the Government's inability in taking action against Mrs Gandhi. He described the Cabinet 'as a group of impotent people.' Meanwhile Raj Narain had addressed a meeting in Shimla in violation of Section 144 and criticised openly Himachal Chief Minister Shanta Kumar. The Cabinet met that evening at Morarji's residence, 1, Safdarjung Road.

All the Ministers except Charan Singh and Raj Narain were present. Raj Narain was in Varanasi. Charan Singh was in Suraj Kund. The Cabinet was informed of the happening. Everyone was aware of the seriousness of the issue. Collective responsibility and Cabinet discipline had been flouted openly. In one voice, the Cabinet authorised Morarji to take whatever action he deemed fit.

Morarji informed the ministers that he would be writing to Charan Singh and Raj Narain requesting them to leave the ministry. Resignation for them was the only way out, if the discipline of the Cabinet had to be maintained, Morarji felt. All the ministers with the exception of Biju Patnaik concurred. Biju also put in a verbal disagreement but went no further.

Morarji shot off letters to Charan Singh and Raj Narain, that evening itself. His Information & Broadcasting Minister

L. K. Advani was told to brief the press. By the time the above mentioned Cabinet meeting took place, Morarji had little option but to ask Charan Singh and Raj Narain to quit. In the preceding months a lot of indiscipline had been tolerated.

Morarji had always been very fair minded in dealing with men and matters. It would not be out of place to quote here an article by P.B. Venkatasubramaniam, which appeared in the *Indian Express* dated 23 November 1989, that amply bears this out.

> *'Those were the early days of the Janata Government. The rumblings of discord within the party, while muted, were audible though the fissures were not apparent. The disastrous blunder of the arrest of Mrs Gandhi with insufficient preparation had been perpetrated followed by her release under the orders of the court.*
>
> *'At that time a well-known advocate who was prominent in the counsels of the ruling party proposed that Mrs Gandhi should be prosecuted on a certain charge. The Prime Minister decided that it should be considered at a meeting and one was convened for that purpose, The papers outlining the proposal were circulated in advance. The meeting was attended among others, by the Home and Law Ministers, the Law Officers headed by the Attorney-General and some Secretaries to the Government, including the Cabinet Secretary. I was one of those present.*
>
> *'The Prime Minister opened the meeting, but when he had just got as far as saying "The proposal is" he*

was interrupted. The interruption came from the Attorney General, the Late S.V. Gupte. Mr Gupte was no friend of Mrs Gandhi, having been strongly critical of her policies at least since the supersession of the three judges in 1973. He was a man of high principles who was to resign his office on the fall of the Desai Government on the ground that he would not be Attorney-General to a government of defectors.

'The interruption was terse and to the point. It was simply "Mr. Prime Minister, that cannot be done. It would not be legal."

'Mr Desai's reaction was equally decisive. He closed his papers and indicated that the matter was closed. Nothing further was heard of the proposal. It was possibly the shortest high level meeting where a decision was taken.

'The advice and the decision alike were characteristic of the persons concerned. The advice was the courageous act of a scrupulously correct person who put the law above prejudice and professional integrity and the demands of his office before expediency and any inclination to please those in power. As regards the decision, it was that of a Prime Minister, who, whatever his other shortcomings, would always uphold the law and permit no deviation from it.'

An Effective Government Falls (1978-79)

By the middle of 1978, the many progressive schemes of the Morarji Government had begun to pay rich dividends. In the year 1978-79, foodgrain production shot up to 130 million tonnes. The five-year plan was reshaped to provide a special emphasis on rural industries and development. As mentioned earlier, the price rise on essential commodities was firmly halted. The rate of inflation was also halted in 1978-79.

One of Morarji's crowning achievements was undoubtedly in the sphere of Foreign Affairs. His government was able to have good relations with Pakistan which touched a new high. President Zia-ul-Haq, who had come to power in the coup of July 1977, was highly impressed by Morarji Desai. Gen Zia felt quite assured with Morarji's genuineness for peace between both the countries. The Foreign Minister A.B. Vajpayee had a successful visit to Pakistan in February, 1978. Morarji met Zia-ul-Haq only once, at the funeral of President Jomo Kenyatta in Nairobi in August, 1978. After the funeral Zia came over to the Nairobi Hilton Hotel where Morarji was staying for a private meeting during which Morarji made a proposition to the military ruler: if both nations acted in a sincere atmosphere of give and take they could avoid unnecessary conflict. To this Zia said that Pakistan was the younger brother and India the elder. Morarji said in a jocular vein that an elder brother could take a younger one to task also. The ice between the two leaders was thus broken and Morarji and Zia were in touch with each other telephonically after that meeting. Zia also sent *maltas* and *kharbuzas* to the Prime Minister in Delhi. Some of Morarji's aides even claim that Zia and Morarji had reached an understanding on Kashmir and it would have been announced on a proposed visit by Morarji to Pakistan. However, the fall of the Janata government scuttled those plans and Zia never had the same equation with the succeeding government of Indira Gandhi. He trusted Morarji and knew he would stand by his word. (*Rediff.com News*, July 2001).

With all other neighbours, Bangladesh, Sri Lanka, Nepal and Bhutan his government got on famously well. India renewed its relationship with China (the Indira Gandhi government had revived diplomatic relations by posting K.R. Narayanan as Ambassador to China in 1976) and in March 1978 a goodwill delegation led by Wang Pin-Nan President of the Chinese People's Association for Friendship with Foreign Countries came to India and was in India for a fortnight. They invited Foreign Minister Vajpayee to visit China. The visit, which took place in February 1979, was, however, controversial as China launched full scale aggression on Vietnam while Vajpayee was still on their soil forcing him to cut short his visit. Vajpayee in his meeting with the Chinese leader Deng Xiaoping told him that India would resent any outside interference in Kashmir and pursue improving relations with Pakistan on the basis of the Shimla Accord. When the news of the Chinese attack on Vietnam became known on 18 February 1979, Morarji immediately issued a statement deploring the Chinese action and called for cessation of hostilities and withdrawal of Chinese troops from the territory of Vietnam. However ill-timed, at least a beginning had been made on the Indo-Sino relationship towards normalisation.

On the internal politics front, by mid-1978, the political tensions in the country were cooling down a bit. The removal of Charan Singh and Raj Narain had virtually gone unprotested, for the simple reason that Morarji had no alternative but to act as he had done at the time. Only a few Ministers of State at the centre like Minister of State Janeshwar Mishra and Narsingh Yadav resigned in protest.

Riots broke out in Aligarh during October 1978 but were controlled fairly quickly. Morarji visited Aligarh shortly after this, met and heard the woes of the riot victims and directed various authorities to speed up relief work. He called for 'ending the game of blaming each other for communal riots,' and asked for 'the cooperation of all sections, to remove this canker.'

Sometimes the in-fighting in the Janata Party came to almost comic proportions. Charan Singh for example, took exception to the speech delivered by the Defence Minister Jagjivan Ram in Bombay, at a function on the 103rd Birth Anniversary of Sardar Patel when he had remarked that the Home Minister of the country had many more important things to attend to than transfer police personnel which was construed as a reference to Charan Singh's tenure in the Ministry of Home Affairs by the press. Charan Singh immediately wrote off a letter on 4 November 1978, saying:

> *'It is since July 1977, that Shri Jagjivan Ram has been attacking me in his public speeches, directly or indirectly. I have kept scrupulously silent. But now my patience has reached the limit. I have decided to hit back. I know this will harm the Janata Party but, then, it appears there is no other recourse left for me.'*

One can well imagine the trying time Morarji must have had keeping the coalition together when senior leaders behaved like schoolchildren! The above letter was a case in point.

November 1978 saw the return of Mrs Gandhi to Parliament from Chikamagalur in Karnataka. It was in November 1978, that the Janata Party held its National Camp at Ujjain. It was here that Morarji made an interesting comment, 'I am neither a yogi nor a commissar,' he had said, probably commenting philosophically on his attitude to life.

The expulsion of Mrs Gandhi from the Lok Sabha took place on 19 December, 1978. It was based on an indictment of the Privileges Committee of Parliament on the Maruti affair. The Committee found that Mrs Gandhi as Prime Minister had prevented officials of the Industrial Development Department from collecting information needed to prepare a reply to a question in the Lok Sabha on the affairs of Maruti Limited, which was the small car project started in the 1970s by her son Sanjay Gandhi. A Privilege Motion in this regard had been moved by Madhu Limaye, MP, on 5 July 1978. It was said in some quarters at that time that Morarji was in favour of milder punishment like suspension from the house for the session. These quarters also suggested that he had a problem of conscience of sending Nehru's daughter to prison. Knowing Morarji personally I do not think this was improbable, however the dictates of coalition politics and the mood of the ruling group in parliament often make the leader do what is in the interest of the political life of the government. Some part of this can be traced in his speech moving the motion for the expulsion of Mrs Gandhi when he said, 'The choice before me and before this House is a very poignant one. In coming to my judgement on that choice I had to set aside my feelings of warmth and affection for her illustrious father and also the memory of my long association with him and her, an association which, but for some erratic interludes has extended over practically the entire period of my political and official career. It is therefore, with a heavy heart, setting aside these personal bonds, that I stand before this House in the discharge of my bounden duty as is the duty of all its members – to protect and preserve its cherished and noble privileges.' The motion was moved by Morarji who, in a landmark speech, said that since Mrs Gandhi had not apologised to the House and had refused to appear before the Privileges Committee, he had no alternative but to take action. He also mentioned that Indira Gandhi was given a full chance to defend herself and examine witnesses before the Parliamentary Committee, her inability to defend herself led her to launch a tirade against the Janata Party. She used diversionary tactics and political polemics to divert attention. 'When Indira Gandhi spoke,' Morarji continued, 'I looked in vain for a trace of remorse or repentance or even self introspection. Every citizen whatever office he or she may have held was equal before the law and one must have the humility to submit himself or herself to the law of the land. No one can claim to be above law,' he said. 'Indira Gandhi,' he went on, 'refused to take oath before the Committee, she was given a full chance to depose without oath and examine witnesses. To all this her answer was an emphatic *No*. The instruments she used to deal with dissenters could be used against her, she could have been arrested or detained or dealt with in a manner as those who used power to destroy democracy have been dealt with by the people or by the government that came to power after their overthrow in various countries, but we did no such thing,' he said.

Certain allegations about Morarji's son Kantilal had surfaced in 1977 and in the monsoon session of parliament in 1978. Charan Singh had also raised them in a letter to the Prime Minister when he was still Home Minister, on 11 March, 1978, on the basis of a speech Morarji was purported to have made in Bhavnagar wherein he was supposed to have talked of an inquiry against his son. Morarji later denied having said so but Charan Singh had written the letter demanding an inquiry. Later after the issue caused an opposition sponsored furore in Parliament during the winter session later in the year a Commission under Justice Vaidyalingam, a former Supreme Court Judge, was set up to inquire whether prima facie cases existed against Kantilal Desai and Charan Singh's family members. The report was published sometime later but except for some inconsequential charges nothing else was found.

On 23 December, 1978, Charan Singh held a large 'Kisan Rally' in Delhi. The Chief Ministers of Uttar Pradesh., Haryana, Bihar and Punjab were present. It was here that Charan Singh, in his speech, floated the idea that the Janata Party should become a federal organisation, that the various groups should revive their original parties, and the governments at the Centre and States should become coalitions. Many of Morarji's colleagues felt that the party should be kept together. Therefore, they prevailed upon him to come to an understanding with Charan Singh. Since this was the view of the majority, as well as the Party President Chandra Shekhar, Morarji agreed to implement their wishes. Morarji later said that his colleagues told him that there was no way out and taking Charan Singh back into the Cabinet was inevitable if the party and government were to survive. However, he put his foot down on the issue of Raj Narain who he felt was too indisciplined to be made a Minister again. He commented, 'I thought at that time that his coming back without Raj Narain was a game, but my friends committed a grave mistake,' (Barun Sengupta, *The Last Days of the Morarji Raj*, 1979).

As a result of the arrangement worked out by Morarji and the other party leaders, Charan Singh rejoined the Cabinet as Deputy Prime Minister on 24 January, 1979, holding charge of the Finance portfolio. The other senior member of the Cabinet, Jagjivan Ram, was also made Deputy Prime Minister and continued to hold charge of the Defence ministry. H.M. Patel who had earlier held the Finance portfolio, was given charge of Home Affairs. Rabi Ray was inducted as Health & Family Welfare Minister. Some other Ministers of State of the BLD group also rejoined the ministry. Not taking back Raj Narain, many feel, was a step which caused the later breakup of the Janata Party. His energies were now fully devoted to bringing down the government. He was bitter at being left out. President Sanjeeva Reddy had also started sending various kinds of letters to Morarji, from end-1978, some of which were later published in 1983. Morarji, always believing in constitutional decorum, replied to all his letters. The President was to play a controversial role in the year to come.

In February 1979, Morarji spent a few days on a Naval Ship *INS Shakti* while visiting the Lakshadweep Islands. The visit was memorable in more ways than one. Vice Admiral M.P. Awati who was the Fleet Commander records that he found that Prime Minister Desai 'held himself erect and spoke Hindi and flawless English with equal facility in a measured tone, as if he had chosen every word with care.' According to the Admiral Morarji visited the engine room and interacted with the officers and sailors and spoke to them about the Navy and its role. He had another crack at jack-staying from one ship to another escorting ship (similar to what he had done in 1977). He told the Fleet Commander that his spoilsport security escorts always cautioned him when he attempted these adventurous escapades! The Jack-staying went off well even though the Fleet Commander was a bit tense till the whole operation was executed. Morarji was tickled a bit when a heavy bag of cement was heaved across the ocean as a pilot preceding his journey across the ocean. A loud cheer went up spontaneously as Morarji waved back to the escort ship on his return to *INS Shakti.* During the evening entertainment programme one of the sailors mimicked Morarji and cracked jokes on his Auto Urine Therapy. Morarji joined in the humour later telling Awati it may have been a little below the belt, but smiled when he was told that it was part of the Naval tradition to encourage earthy, nautical humour. Awati was to remark that here was an 'affable person, if there was one.' During the first few months of 1979, the domestic scene was quite gratifying for Morarji. As his government completed its second year in office, the earlier tempo of keeping prices down, maintaining good law and order and successful foreign policy had been kept up. In February 1979, foreign Minister Vajpayee paid a visit to China. The Chinese attack on Vietnam, which was coincidental, forced him to abandon his visit, but during the Janata rule a thaw was appearing in India's relations with China regarding the territories occupied in 1962.

On 9 March, 1979, Soviet Prime Minister Alexei Kosygin came to India and another milestone in Indo-Soviet friendship was reached. In March 1979, Jaya Prakash Narayan fell critically ill (his kidneys were failing) and he was rushed to Bombay by an Air Force Plane. On the 23rd March, Morarji was informed by the Director, Intelligence Bureau S.N. Mathur that JP had succumbed to his illness. Morarji accordingly informed Parliament which was adjourned after tributes were paid. Soon after news was received that JP was still alive and that the news received was false as a mix-up had taken place in Bombay. Morarji informed the House and apologised for the announcement made on the basis of wrong information supplied to him.

In April 1979, Morarji made a tour of Bangladesh, which helped in promoting his policy of good relations with the neighbours. He had been to Sri Lanka earlier in the year.

In March-April 1979, the BLD and Socialist elements within the Janata Party began to bring up the 'dual membership issue on the plea that members of the Jan Sangh group, who were also members of the RSS (Rashtriya Swayamsevak Sangh) should sever their links with this organisation as the Janata was a secular party. However, by the end of May and around early June 1979, things seemed to be calm for the Janata Government, at least outwardly. The saying that, 'There is a calm before the storm' was particularly true of the early summer of 1979.

Earlier, in 1979, two BLD group Chief Ministers Ram Naresh Yadav of Uttar Pradesh and Karpoori Thakur of Bihar were asked to seek a 'vote of confidence' in their States by Janata Parliamentary Board, on the complaints of legislators. Both of them lost. Banarsi Dass and Ram Sunder Das were elected as Chief Ministers of Uttar Pradesh and Bihar respectively. This had, to an extent, heightened the tensions within the Janata Government, but by May-June 1979 things were quite calm on the surface, as mentioned earlier. Morarji, as one magazine commented, 'was reaping a rich political harvest.'

However, the destabilising effect of frequent changes in the State governments had an effect on the centre as well. The BLD group and the Socialists had in March-April begun raising the issue of the Jan Sangh members of the Janata Party having dual membership of the Right Wing Hindu Voluntary Organisation. Although this situation had been prevailing since 1977, it did indeed give the Charan Singh group a stick to beat the party leadership with. Both sides were not willing to go in for a compromise. It led to a showdown which ultimately proved fatal for the Janata Party and government. The RSS had always had the undertones of a religious militant outfit and its leaders had been indicted by various Commissions of Inquiry to be connected with instigating riots in various parts of the country at various times be it at Jabalpur or Ahmedabad or other places. Later the RSS Chief Balasaheb Deoras gave an assurance that Jan Sangh members would not take part in day to day functioning of the RSS, but by then the die was cast.

Moreover, behind the scenes, a conspiracy was being hatched, the results of which would be unfolded in the weeks to come. In June 1979, Morarji embarked on a tour of the Soviet Union and some Eastern Bloc countries. It was to be his last foreign tour as Prime Minister.

On 10 June, 1979, he arrived at Tashkent to a cheering reception. A spontaneous burst of emotion greeted him as the people of Tashkent warmly cheered him all the way from the airport to his villa. The crowds and welcomes were to swell as the visit progressed.

While at Tashkent he laid wreaths at the tomb of the Unknown Soldier and the mausoleum of Lenin and later strolled down the streets of Tashkent. On coming across a huge portrait of Brezhnev on the sidewalk, Morarji said 'Oh! Such a big portrait.' A Russian security officer told him, 'Sir, this is

Comrade Brezhnev.' To which Morarji is said to have quipped, 'So it had to be big.' An official from Morarji's party said in hushed tones, 'Big brother is watching.' Morarji turned and smiled at him.

The rest of the day in Tashkent was spent visiting the dacha where Prime Minister Lal Bahadur Shastri had died and the Institute of Religious Studies at Taskhent.

On 11 June, a special Aeroflot jetliner took Morarji to Moscow, where President Brezhnev broke protocol yet again and came to receive him. He greeted Morarji with open arms and Muscovites lined whole route from the Airport to the Kremlin. It was one of the biggest welcomes the Soviets had given to a visiting dignitary.

President Brezhnev had talks with Morarji stretching over two days for three-and-a-half hours, which was usually reserved only for heads of state. Morarji got an assurance from Brezhnev that India's relations with the Soviet Union would not be affected in the event of improvement in Sino-Soviet relations. Supply of additional crude and an integrated new steel plant at Vishakhapatnam were part of the package worked out during the visit.

As a return courtesy to President Brezhnev's banquet in his honour, Morarji hosted a lunch in honour of Soviet Premier Alexei Kosygin.

An interesting sidelight to the visit: One evening when Morarji was out of his room in the Kremlin, one of his aides removed some cotton bits which were lying on the sofa where Morarji had been spinning his charkha and put them in the waste-paper basket. On returning, Morarji asked where the cotton bits had gone. On being told, he went and retrieved them from the waste-paper basket himself. 'Nothing should be wasted,' he is said to have remarked.

After Moscow, Leningrad was his next stop, where Morarji was able to see the 'white night.' During the months of June and July the street lights of Leningrad are switched off so that people could see the 'white night.'

It was here that Prime Minister Morarji saw the gunboat *Aurora* berthed on the Neva River from where a shot was fired to herald the Russian Revolution. Lenin had proclaimed the success of the revolution from here.

While at Leningrad, Morarji visited the small room from where Lenin had conducted the revolution and saw some personal belongings of Lenin. He also witnessed a ballet at Kirov's Opera and Ballet Theatre.

Before his departure from Leningrad he visited the Hermitage Museum which was once the winter palace of the Czars. After Leningrad Morarji left for Poland to spend two days in Warsaw. After Warsaw his next stop was Prague, Czechoslovakia. The Communist Party Chief Gustav Husak not only broke protocol to meet Morarji, but accorded him a 21-gun salute. He had talks with the Czech leaders and attended a dinner in the evening.

Morarji next arrived in Belgrade and, after conferring with Yugoslav Premier Veselin Djuranvovic, left on the morning of 19 June, to meet President Tito at the island of Brioni. President Tito was waiting for Morarji at the jetty of Brioni. A red carpet was laid out and as Morarji and Tito walked on it, to the nearby Guest house, young girls spread rose petals on their path. Later Morarji had another round of talks with Tito at his villa near the White Palace and as Tito got up to leave he asked Morarji not to take the trouble of coming out to see him off. To this, Morarji said, 'You are elder to me.' This touched Tito and he embraced him.

With a few hours halt at Frankfurt, Morarji returned home. His visit brought India very much close to the countries of the communist Bloc.

On arrival back home, Morarji found the situation within the ruling party fairly critical, but it did not look as if any storm was in the offing. In the meantime the Janata Parliamentary Board directed another Chief Minister, Devi Lal of Haryana to seek a vote of confidence, which he lost. Bhajan Lal took over as the next Chief Minister. Groupism between the BLD and Jan Sangh groups was taking place in right earnest after the second week of June. Delhi was rife with the talk of many a conspiracy to topple the Morarji Government.

It was on 26 June that Raj Narain bolted from the Janata Party. A resolution for his expulsion due to anti-party activities was pending before the National Executive. But it did not seem at that time that this was much of a threat to the Desai government. On 2 July, Deputy Prime Minister Charan Singh announced that he and Raj Narain had 'finally' parted company. The events of the next few days were to prove something totally different.

On 9 July, 1979, the Monsoon Session of Parliament began. On that day itself the flow to Raj Narain's group started. Members of Parliament (MP) crossed over that morning. By 11th July, Morarji's government lost its majority on the floor of the Lok Sabha as more MPs defected. Morarji at that time had expressed confidence that his government would ride the storm, even though as always, he was not interested in making any compromise to stay in power. On 12 July, three Ministers – Rabi Ray, Janeshwar Mishra and Jagbir Singh – resigned. The Jan Sangh meanwhile offered to support the government from outside by withdrawing its Ministers from the Ministry as there were indications that the rebel group would support the government in that event. The 'dual membership' issue had been raised predominantly by the Raj Narain group. Morarji, however, turned down the offer as he felt it incorrect to surrender to such blackmail of the rebel group. He also said that he felt the Jan Sangh had not conducted itself properly on some matters.

On the same day, 12th July, Morarji's Industry Minister, George Fernandes, pulverised the opposition attack with a hard-hitting speech on the floor of the Lok Sabha defending the Janata Government. The speech was full of facts and figures. However, by the 14th of July, George Fernandes, Biju Patnaik and H.N. Bahuguna left the Cabinet. The rebel group had swelled to 75 MPs.

The voting on the No-Confidence Motion which had been tabled by the leader of the opposition Y.B. Chavan was to take place on Monday, the 16 July 1979. At the meeting of the Parliamentary Board, on the 14th July, Morarji was confident that the Government would survive the No-Confidence Motion as a large number of Congress MPs would abstain.

However, by the evening of 15th July the die was cast. It was clear that the government would not survive the No Confidence

Motion. Morarji, after long consultations with his colleagues, resigned on the evening of 15th July 1979 as Prime Minister of India. However, he made it clear to President Reddy that the Janata Party still was the single largest party in the Lok Sabha and should therefore, be allowed to explore the possibility of forming the next government.

In a statement issued after resigning, Morarji said, 'I hope the nation will strengthen the hands of all those who stand for principles and values, all those who rise above petty differences, resolve to give the country a strong and stable progressive government. I have full confidence in the future of our great country.' On 18th July, President Reddy asked the leader of the opposition Y.B. Chavan to explore the possibility of forming a government.

By 22nd July, Chavan reported back to the President that he was not in a position to form a government, but an axis with Charan Singh who had quit the caretaker government was being worked out, he told the President. By now the whole game-plan of the Raj Narain-Charan Singh group which was named the Janata(S) became clear. Charan Singh was out to fulfil his life's ambition.

On 23rd July, President Reddy called both Charan Singh and Morarji to explore the possibility of forming a government. It was an unprecedented step that two persons should be invited to form a government. Morarji made it clear to the President that he would require an extra day, as the President had asked for proof of support by 25th July, 4:00 pm. The President agreed to it.

However, on the morning of 25th July, the President told Morarji that the list would have to be submitted that day itself and an extra day, which had been earlier agreed to, could not be given. Morarji's list was thus submitted under pressure of time. Also since he was shouldering responsibilities of a caretaker government, he could not devote enough time to checking the list and left it to others in the party.

On 26th July, President Reddy invited Charan Singh to form the next government, on the basis of his having a larger number of names in his list. Later Morarji was to comment on the President's conduct during the crisis, 'It is an extraordinary way in which he has functioned. That is all I can say. Can two people be called at the same time to form a government? Can anybody be called to form a government without a majority? And it is obvious from the letter it is not so ... I had asked for one more day (to submit the list) from the President. He had first agreed. But after that he changed his mind and said it would have to be before 4:00 pm the same day. So I did not want to quibble about it. Why should I? For example, when I was going to speak on the All India Radio he phoned me and asked "What are you doing? This is not right." I asked, "How is it not right?" "You are a caretaker government" he said. What is a caretaker government? There is no word like caretaker in the Constitution – a government is a government. I was not doing anything else. I was only giving reasons for my resignation.' (Interview to *India Today*, 31 Aug 1979).

There is little doubt that Sanjeeva Reddy was playing a patently political role during the 1979 crisis. Was it that he had political ambitions of his own to emerge as a consensus candidate for the Prime Ministership?

On his last day in office Morarji was remarkably composed when the news came in that Charan Singh had been invited to form the government. He did not leave a scrap of paper pending on his desk and attended to all pending matters including meeting the departing Portuguese Ambassador. Nearly 50 years earlier while leaving the service of the British Government's Provincial Service he had cleared all pending work on his desk, it was therefore, in the fitness of things that while leaving his last political office as Prime Minister he followed the same principle.

Morarji issued a statement the next day announcing his retirement from active politics and resigned as leader of the Janata Parliamentary Party. He felt he should atone for the lapse of submitting a list which contained the names of some of the MPs from the Congress who did not support him. Morarji felt that even though the list was made under tremendous time pressure, he should take full responsibility for the errors. The letter of resignation as leader of the Janata Parliamentary Party (JPP), written by him to the Party President Chandra Shekhar is reproduced below. It was a well-drafted letter, written beautifully, capturing the mood of those days.

> *'I have been pondering over the events of the last few days and have been considering the duty that I owe to myself, the party and the country at this hour.*
>
> *'We have all been condemning defection in no uncertain terms and have reiterated our determination to prevent it by legislation. No one even in his wildest imagination could however have considered that defection would take place in*

the manner in which it did and the grounds on which such defections were sought to be justified. One had come to overlook much that was improper and unprincipled. But I cannot help the feeling that what occurred during the past few days brought us down to the lowest possible level of political conduct and behaviour. Utter cynicism held full sway.

'In such an atmosphere, I have been particularly concerned at the allegation that I had been responsible for deliberate falsehood by including some names from the Congress party among the list of my supporters. It was my intention to subject every name to careful scrutiny before presenting it to the President. I thought I had time to do so as I had thought that I had been given one more day by the President on the 23rd at my request and that I could submit the list on the 26th.

'On the 25th morning however, the President insisted that the list be submitted that very afternoon by 4:00 pm and refused to give me the extra day asked for, even though he told me on the 23rd that I could take one more day when I asked for it. However, the fact remains that under pressure of time I submitted a list over my signature which included the names of those who, in the event, turned out not to have agreed to support my government. I must take full responsibility and blame for this even though I could urge that the including had not been made at my instance.

'I have after deep reflection come to the conclusion that I at least should not in any way contribute to this atmosphere

of our political life. I have decided that it is my moral duty to atone for this lapse and I accordingly resign from the leadership of the Janata Parliamentary Party. I shall not hereafter take part in any political activity. I am also giving thought to the advisability of resigning from the Lok Sabha.'

After Morarji's resignation, Jagjivan Ram became leader of the Janata Parliamentary Party (JPP). Within a few weeks of the new government taking over, Morarji vacated his Delhi residence and shifted to Bombay.

Later Morarji expressed his views about the President's decision emphatically, saying that it had set a bad precedent unheard of in a democracy that two people should be invited to form a government and parade supporters. As a President so concerned about the falling standards in public life Sanjeeva Reddy egged horse-trading by adopting this procedure. One of the reasons for Sanjeeva Reddy's hostility to Morarji Desai was his Secretary Maddappa whom Sanjeeva Reddy wanted to be appointed as Comptroller and Auditor General. Morarji had expressed his inability to do so. In private conversation Morarji used to say, 'Making Sanjeeva Reddy President was my greatest mistake as Prime Minister.' As expected, the Charan Singh Ministry resigned in 24 days, on 20 August, 1979. Charan Singh became the only Prime Minister who never faced Parliament for a single day. The Congress (I), Charan Singh's ally, had withdrawn support.

Ignoring the claims of JPP leader Jagjivan Ram, President Reddy dissolved the Lok Sabha and called for a mid-term poll.

Life in Retirement

Although Morarji was 83 years old when he resigned as Prime Minister, he was much fitter than many a younger person. He could even at that age run up a flight of stairs. As mentioned earlier, since 1975, he had been living only on uncooked food and milk. He took only two meals a day for many years, one at 9:45 am and the other at 6:45 pm. His meals consisted of fresh fruit, dry fruit, cottage cheese and some cucumber, carrot, all in limited quantities. His evening meal was lighter, accompanied by a jug of warm milk. In between meals he used to take coconut water in the afternoons.

After resigning in 1979, he actively campaigned for his party even after the Congress returned to power. Like always, he met a lot of people, ranging from ordinary folks to the wealthy and powerful who came to his residence at Bombay. Till he died in 1995, at the age of 99, he used to meet a variety of people who called at his residence. For him, it was of paramount importance to render service to his countrymen. Once while asked by a journalist, what brought him the greatest pleasure, Morarji said, 'Bringing a smile to someone's face. Because that is what enables a person to be free of burden, free of anger, free of excitement.'

In the summer of 1983 an event which created some ripples concerning Morarji Desai took place in relation to a book published in the United States titled *The Price of Power: Kissinger in the Nixon White House* written by Pulitzer Prize winning journalist Seymour Hersh. Hersh in the volume alleged that Morarji was receiving $ 20,000 from the CIA from the time of the Johnson Presidency till the early 1970s. The relevant extract from the book was as follows, 'The source was never named in the Kissinger and Nixon memoirs for an obvious reason: the informant was reporting from India through the CIA. Nixon and Kissinger may have been honourable in protecting the man, but the few in American Government who knew his identity must also have known that his identity was highly biased. The informant was undoubtedly Morarji Desai who was fired from the post of Deputy Prime Minister in 1969 ... Desai was a paid informer for the CIA and considered one of the agency's important assets. Former American officials report that Desai was a star performer who was paid $20,000 a year by the CIA during the Lyndon B. Johnson's administration through the 303 Committee the covert intelligence group that was replaced by the 40 Committee under Nixon and Kissinger ... I have been able to establish firmly that Desai was reporting through 1970.'

These allegations caused an uproar in the Indian media and in Parliament. Nobody, even those who were on the other side of the political spectrum from Desai, believed the allegations. The then Prime Minister, Indira Gandhi, however, was not emphatic in denying the charge except an off-the-cuff statement at an airport press conference where she said, 'I hope the allegation is not true.' This did cause some disquiet among right thinking people who believed that Hersh's charge amounted to accusing the Pope of having a mistress and the government of the day and the Prime Minister should have risen above party politics and come out clearly in denial when the name of an elder statesman had been sullied. *The Times of India* at that time put it succinctly which conveyed the national sentiment, '*Everything we have known about Mr Desai given his long record of dedicated service to the country, his self righteousness and pride ... assert and affirm his singular inability to engage in secret activity.*'

Even though Hersh alleged that Morarji was pro-America and anti-Soviet Union in his outlook, the facts speak differently. Morarji in 1968 as Deputy Prime Minister, had according to the Cabinet papers of the period, strongly objected when Indira Gandhi was seriously considering signing the American Non Proliferation Treaty, which was then shelved; he also protested against the CIA sponsored joint project to place a fresh nuclear test monitoring device on Nanda Devi after the original was buried by a snowstorm. Apart from this he also insisted (as a member of the Indira Cabinet) for the termination of the 1959 agreement with the CIA for training of Khampa rebels to ambush Chinese convoys 10 years after it was signed. From these few examples mentioned it is clear as daylight that a person who was able to take such a strong stand against America could hardly be on the payroll of the CIA.

Hersh made several mistakes in his account such as that Morarji had continued in the Cabinet throughout 1970 and reported on the 1971 war, whereas he had quit the Indira Cabinet in July 1969. Hersh also mentioned that Mrs Gandhi assumed office as Prime Minister in July 1979 but in reality she made her comeback in January 1980.

He also stated that Morarji Desai was reporting to the CIA during the Johnson administration but during the four years of that administration from 1964 to 1968 Desai was in political limbo under the Kamaraj Plan and returned to the Cabinet only in 1967 during the final year of the Johnson administration. It is also difficult to believe that a Cabinet Minister would have passed on information for a paltry $20,000 punching another hole in Hersh's story. Charan Singh and Gulzarilal Nanda, both former Home Ministers (the former having held the portfolio under Morarji as we have seen earlier), immediately dismissed the charges as fake in 1983, but Jagjivan Ram who had been Deputy Prime Minister in the Janata Government and had been a colleague of Desai in various Ministries declined to comment at the time, leaving many an observer wondering why he did so.

Morarji at that time described the allegation as '*a slur on the country, which the government should deny, it is mischievous of them to remain silent.*' Public opinion at the time also generally supported his viewpoint. Although he initially did not express a desire to do so, Morarji did file a case in a Chicago Court for libel for $ 3.5 million (₹5.5 Crore). He travelled to the US twice in 1984 and 1985 to depose in the US Court. His final testimony in 1989 had to be videotaped as he was by then too unwell to travel. Unfortunately in America to win a libel suit the plaintiff must show that not only is the offending statement false but also that the writer either knew it to be false or did not care whether it was true or not. It therefore becomes extremely difficult for a litigant, that too from another country, to prove his case. In this also the court exempted Seymour Hersh from disclosing his sources. Thus even though the Former United States Secretary of State Henry Kissinger and CIA Director Richard Helms testified under oath that Morarji had never acted for the CIA or been paid anything the Chicago Court on 6 October 1989 acquitted Hersh of the charges. Morarji took the verdict with his usual stoicism, with the comment to the press that his character did not depend or change on what the American judiciary thought of him. Rightly, he decided not to appeal as the US Libel laws stacked the odds against him. Also his inability to appear in person would have affected the case further not favouring him.

However, the author hopes that one day the real truth of the absurd and malicious allegation comes to light.

In this connection the author would like to state an interesting incident. Some years later, when the author was having a private conversation with B.K. Nehru at his residence in Kasauli, he mentioned to the author that he was convinced that one M.J. Desai, who was Secretary General in the Ministry of External Affairs, was very pro American in his dealings and it was probable that he may have been involved with the CIA. On further probing, B.K. Nehru refused to say anything further except, 'I am convinced in the matter.' The author hastens to add that he has no proof of M.J. Desai's involvement. However he would like to underline the fact that B.K. Nehru, having served for many years in the US as the Indian Ambassador, would not have made the comment without basis or firm belief. A further point he would like to highlight was that B.K. Nehru was very close to Morarji having been Secretary in the Department of Economic Affairs when Morarji was Finance Minister.

Till 1988, Morarji did quite a bit of touring throughout this vast country. Even in the 1984 Lok Sabha elections he toured the northern and southern states, though he was almost 89 years of age at the time. Nature Cure also helped him maintain his health. Since 1915 he had not taken any allopathic medicine whatsoever. He was till the end very alert for a man of his age. His memory was also good.

In 1988, President Zia-ul-Haq of Pakistan conferred on Morarji Desai, Pakistan's highest civilian award, the 'Nishan-e-Pakistan' for his outstanding contribution to Indo-Pak relations. A grateful nation on 26 January, 1991 honoured itself by conferring on Morarji, who can undoubtedly be regarded as one of modern India's most illustrious sons, the Bharat Ratna.

Since 1988, Morarji did not go out of his residence, mainly on account of his advanced age. He used to read 15 newspapers everyday in English and Gujarati. As mentioned earlier he remained very alert for his age till the end.

As his hundredth year approached, though enfeebled with age, Morarji continued with his daily routine as always and was mentally as alert as ever. On 28 February 1995 a grand function was held in the terrace hall of his apartment complex – 'Sarang' in South Mumbai. The eminent lawyer and former Ambassador to the USA Nani Palkhivala was presiding and spoke eloquently as was usual with him about the contribution of Morarji in the political realm including his achievements as a Prime Minister.

Shortly thereafter Morarji was admitted to Jaslok Hospital in Mumbai where he was diagnosed with a blood clot in the brain for which he was operated upon. Old age and bodily weakness had however taken their toll and on 10 April 1995, the warrior of many a battle lost the battle against mortality. Two days later, his final journey on this earth took place at Ahmedabad, the very city where he began his career in the Provincial Civil Service many a decade back. His Memorial, known as Abhay Ghat, is on the banks of the Sabarmati River very close to the Sabarmati Ashram of Mahatma Gandhi who was Morarji Desai's mentor and in many ways the guiding spirit in Morarji's life.

The Many Shades and Hues of Morarji Desai

It is now 24 years since Morarji Desai passed away, on 10 April 1995. The younger generation may not wholly remember him but it is doubtful if he has been or could have been wholly forgotten by any generation young or old. There are reasons both in the ideological and historical perspective of things.

Firstly, the government he headed assumed office in circumstances which were unique in the history of the Indian republic, for it came in after ousting a dictatorial regime. The damage done to the Constitution by the 42nd Amendment (which Nani Palkhivala described as that 'monstrous outrage' on the Constitution) had to be undone, the bureaucracy had to be put on the rails after the total disregard for norms which had prevailed during the previous nineteen months of authoritarian rule bordering on anarchy.

Secondly, he is remembered as a man who did not mind calling a spade a spade and never considering himself in the popularity race. For example he voiced his views against the previous government's takeover of Sikkim unequivocally in Parliament even though he received virtually no support from his own party during the course of the debate.

One of his lasting achievements was making another Declaration of Emergency virtually impossible by amending the Constitution by the 44th Amendment Act which had the unmistakable stamp of Morarji Desai's thinking as a democrat and a man with a vision. This Amendment provided that henceforth an Emergency could be declared on Armed Rebellion alone and not on Internal Disturbance as was earlier provided. Another important feature of this Amendment was that it made the Fundamental Rights a feature of the Constitution which could not be suspended under an Emergency, which was previously allowed under the Constitution. The state of Internal Emergency could henceforth only be declared on the written advice of the Cabinet. (The 1975 emergency declaration had been signed on the midnight of 25 June 1975 by President Fakhruddin Ali Ahmed and the Cabinet was informed post facto). This 44th Amendment did not, however, remove the words 'secular' and 'socialist' which had been inserted into the Preamble by the 42nd Amendment. Though small this was a very significant part of 44th Amendment as it secured to future generations the secular and socialist nature of the republic. At least on paper no future regime can easily change these basic tenets of the Constitution. It goes to the credit of Morarji Desai and his Law Minister Shanti Bhushan that they were open minded enough not to disturb Amendments passed by the previous regime which were in the larger national interest. On being once asked as to what he felt was the single most important achievement of the Janata Government he said, 'removing the sense of fear from the hearts of the people. They were terrified by what they saw was happening around them during the Emergency and they were too scared to come out openly. We changed all that. We brought the spirit of democracy back to the land.' The well known journalist and writer Kuldip Nayar was of the view that the most lasting achievement of Morarji and the Janata Party government is that an Emergency through the back door as in 1975 was now virtually impossible. He is on record as having said, 'This Constitutional coup can never be repeated.'

In the year 1984 the author had a fairly extensive conversation with Morarji Desai at his apartment in Marine Drive in Mumbai. The notes made at that time based on these interactions provided insights into the multi-faceted personality of Morarji and gave the author glimpses into the many facets of his character – his personality, principles, ideals and ideologies, his views on various issues like education, prohibition, public sector and private sector, his thoughts on his political colleagues, partners and opponents. In the following paragraphs, the author would like to share with the readers snippets from the conversations he had had with Morarji and information gleaned by the author from other sources as well to sum up this biography with an overview of Morarji Desai as a person, as an idealist, as an administrator and highlight how the idealist lived by his principles and ideologies and how he tried his very best to contributing to building an India of his dreams.

Personal Beliefs, Ideals and Faiths

In Morarji's life, the Bhagvad Gita had occupied a very prominent place. In the year 1934, he committed the whole

Gita to memory and began to recite it once or twice daily and this deepened his faith in God and the Gita with every passing day. As the law of action and reaction exists in Physics, so says Morarji, exists the Law of Karma in Spiritual Science. The ambit of Spiritual Science is very much larger than the Physical one. The Universe, he feels, is under this everlasting law of God, which is all pervading and every being has to receive the result of karma, without exception. He was fully committed to his belief in the Law of Karma as enunciated in the Gita. Even when writhing in pain he did not make a sound as he believed it was connected to his past karma.

It is his great faith in God which gave Morarji complete peace of mind and made him such a calm and unruffled person. Morarji had said once that he 'had no desire of any kind except the desire of trying to understand truth and to realise it and follow it.' It is this which has been his main thrust throughout his life.

Morarji was a great believer in destiny, which again he felt was linked to the Law of Karma. He believed as the Gita says that one should neither be overjoyed by success, nor be despondent on failure. Both these should be treated with equanimity. Morarji felt that the future generations should not forget India's glorious culture and heritage, which he believed was something unique.

A word about Morarji's family may not be out of place here. After 1930 he had three surviving children: his daughter Virumati, second daughter Indu and his son Kantilal. Virumati, married to Ramanlal Desai, passed away in early 2000s. His second daughter Indu, who was a medical student, unfortunately committed suicide in 1953 after being jilted by the man she was due to marry. Kantilal, who has been mentioned earlier, had been in business and was later Morarji's Private Secretary passed away in September 2014. His wife Padma who belonged to the Kirloskar family also sadly committed suicide in 1984. Morarji bore all these tragedies with equanimity.

Few people know that Morarji Desai the great disciplinarian was a smoker in his younger days (probably while in Government Service in the 1920s). He said once that he smoked in his younger days but then gave it up. (Interview with Pritish Nandy, *The Illustrated Weekly of India*, 2 February, 1986.)

It is often said that Morarji Desai was a rigid person who did not entertain any other point of view on certain issues and had a one-track mind. While the author is willing to concede that he held strong views on certain subjects like prohibition and pacifism which included India not developing Nuclear Weapons, to use the term rigid with regard to Morarji is being grossly unfair to the man. The late S. Nihal Singh, in conversation with the author, had stated that according to him Morarji was a fairly gentle soul whose outward exterior of being a person of strong beliefs often led him to be thought of as rigid and stubborn. Nihal Singh found him interested in various things of life as well. D.F. Karaka's views were that Morarji lacked tact at times and had an innate shyness which was often misunderstood. Those who worked with Morarji closely are on record affirming that it was possible to argue with him thus appealing to his innate sense of fair play and make him alter his view. Morarji did not make any attempt to play to the gallery and woo the public through populist moves or speech. He considered it his duty in public to do what was in the best interest of the nation. To that extent he may have viewed the masses as fumblers who had to be shown the right way. One example was his view expressed in an interview to the *New York Times* on the takeover of Sikkim by the previous Indira Gandhi government which he condemned as undesirable. Later when the issue arose in Parliament he stated that his views were nothing new and had been expressed before he became the Prime Minister. It was an example of his not being in the popularity race.

Morarji did not believe in leaving the field when the chips were down. When his government fell in 1979, he made the following comment, 'For me there is no choice except to follow the path of duty as I see it. It is easy to leave, but it is very difficult to remain in position and meet the challenge ... I have never looked for soft options or compromised on principles for the sake of any personal gain. They were available to me in 1964, 1966, 1967, 1969 and are available even now. But they are not for me. I will do what is in the best interest of the nation. If, in the process, I have to make any personal sacrifice, neither my Party nor my country will find me wanting.'

Morarji was a great believer in the future of India. 'I am always an optimist,' he used to say. He felt that the nation would move ahead in various spheres in the years to come. Slowly, age old differences of caste and creed will disappear and people would forget these narrow confines dividing mankind.

Throughout his long life, whether it was leaving the PCS or resigning as Prime Minister, Morarji had never for a minute compromised with the principles he had held dear. Contentment was also one of the great qualities of Morarji Desai. He was committed, content and always selfless in his thoughts.

On the Mahatma

Morarji's views on the Mahatma were quite unambiguous. Morarji believed that: 'Gandhi's greatest strength was that he always stuck to truth as he saw it. He persisted with an image of his own irrespective of what anyone else thought of it. He never asked anyone else to do something he would not do himself, thus his greatest power was his popularity with the masses and the strength of his political movement came from earnest support.' Whilst on the subject it is interesting to note that in his early political career Morarji had mentioned to Gandhi that he should give up the habit of leaning on two women while walking as even though he had great self control others might misuse this style of walking. Even though Gandhiji did not concede the rightness of Morarji's argument, he later did make mention of it in an article in the *Harijan* accepting the validity of Morarji's view on the basis of the behaviour of a certain political worker. This led some scribes to comment that Morarji had delivered a homily even to the Mahatma!

On Prohibition

Morarji was always a great votary of Prohibition as he felt that only 20% of the Indian population was given to the vice of drinking; and 80% of this drinking populace are the poverty stricken masses. This vice affects their health, their morals and their entire life as also that of their family and dependants.

He believed that Prohibition could be easily implemented and enforced in India if the necessary political will existed in those governing the nation.

Morarji was of the view that liquor had caused many crimes, broken up homes and caused immeasurable hardships particularly among women and children. He once said in an interview. 'Drinking is worse than a crime, it is the mother of all crimes. Wine and women go together. Hardly any drunkard can have any character, for he is not responsible for what he does.' It was only his deep feeling of pain for the suffering millions of our country that had prompted him to pursue the Prohibition policy time and again which he felt was without doubt practical and implementable.

Morarji felt that in India the chances of success of prohibition were much more favourable than in any other country. Drinking was against ancient Indian culture and ethos. The percentage of people drinking was still very low. However, he was of the view that the Government should take proper steps to curtail drinking becoming a general habit among the public for that would be a great disaster for a nation where the people have a general aversion to intoxicants.

Also, Morarji felt, one must look at the economic aspect of the problem since a large number of poor people in our country are known to spend 60 to 70% of their income or more on consuming liquor. It makes life hell for them. It is therefore, imperative if we are to rise the living standard of our people that liquor booths should be done away with and prohibition imposed.

Prohibition formed a very prominent part of the Congress Party's policy under the leadership of Mahatma Gandhi during the freedom struggle right since 1928 when it was adopted at the Calcutta Session of the AICC. The Mahatma had appealed to all the Congress Ministries which came to power in the provinces in 1937 to implement Prohibition with full force. Morarji also pointed out that the Indian Constituent Assembly had also unanimously voted for including Prohibition in the Directive Principles. Like the outlawing of thieving, betting and cheating, prohibition of intoxicants was necessary for the betterment of society as a whole. Morarji also felt that illegal distillation of liquor would definitely not go up if Prohibition was enforced properly.

It would be in the fitness of things to mention here a quote from Gandhiji which Morarji mentioned in one of his speeches. 'Drugs and drink are the two arms of the devil with which he strikes his helpless slaves into stupefaction and intoxication. The drinking and drug evil in many respects is infinitely worse than the evil of malaria and the like, for whilst the latter only injures the body, the former saps both body and soul.'

On Education

Education was a subject close to Morarji's heart. He felt that proper development of education is vital for the progress of any country, much more so for a country like India where millions and millions of people had been denied the opportunities of education. At least 30% of government expenditure should be in the field of education, he is once reported to have said.

He felt that education must be in line with the progressing social order in the country to promote equality of opportunity and human status in the society. It should be in line with the social order the Constitution seeks to create and therefore, should be aimed at the elimination of special privileges for a section of society.

Morarji was of the view that India would do well to remember Gandhiji's ideal of 'Basic Education.' The Mahatma had experimented with work-oriented education at Phoenix and Tolstoy Farms during his stay in South Africa. Development of India's rich regional languages as well as 'Hindustani' was what the Mahatma laid emphasis on.

Morarji felt that India's Constitution makers rightly provided that education should be on the Concurrent List so that both the Centre and the States can legislate on it. This according to him was in the fitness of things and promoted the national ideal of unity in diversity. He felt that development of elementary education must be the primary focus when thinking of or formulating policies on education.

He felt that there should be no divisions or gradations like Senior level, Junior level, etc. and there should just be middle schooling and Senior or Pre-University level of Schooling. He also held the view that certain Public Schools in the country which existed only to impart education to the children of the rich and super rich and had in the process become mini-pockets of aristocracy should be done away with as they had become one of the key instruments in accelerating economic and social disparities within the people.

According to him, the concept of a uniform system of education was more attuned to and in line with Indian needs. Teachers' training, he maintained, was a very important aspect of education. Teachers had to be alive to their inherent duties. It was important that the training inculcated in the teachers the qualities of devotion, integrity, patriotism and social service.

Morarji also subscribed to the view that at the University level of education full autonomy and freedom must be given to the Universities for their functioning and to maintain their distinct character and past tradition. He was equally emphatic that development of Hindi and the regional languages should be given pre-dominance in India's Education Policy. Further, he felt that education had to be of paramount importance in the scheme of national reconstruction.

He believed that the education system in India required drastic change and blamed the British system of education for it. Education in his view had to be such as to inculcate self respect, love for truth and dignity of labour broadly. (Also mentioned in an interview with *India Today*, 31 August 1979 'We have no pride in our country – that is our misfortune – particularly amongst the educated. They are a liability in this country – because of the education – I don't find fault with them. After all, if one is educated that way what can you do? It is the British Government's education system which we have not changed ... I was trying to tackle education. I came to a point where I would have implemented it in six months.')

On Administration and Governance

Morarji once said that, 'I am a rightist in the sense that I believe in doing what is right.' Although called a great exponent of free enterprise he was basically a supporter of mixed economy with support to free enterprise up to a limit. This view of his he made clear when he said, 'Too much opening up is also not good. Free competition is good but only up to a point. There are some sectors which can function best under direct government control ... if you allow free rein to the private sector in every area the common man will be exploited.' (Interview with Pritish Nandy, *The Illustrated Weekly of India*, 2 February, 1986)

He was fairly enthusiastic about the Public Sector which he believed could co-exist with the Private Sector and was of the opinion that experts in various fields should be inducted into Public Sector units to make them more productive. The tenure of these persons inducted should be short term and not with a kind of permanence as security tends to lead to inefficiency.

On Trade Unions he had a positive view but added the stipulation that the unions and union leaders would be useful to the workers and the country only and only if they truly worked in the workers' interests, were just in the demands made by them and did not resort to politics and moves aimed at personal gains.

Morarji always gave greater thought to improve the tone of government administration. He felt that it was necessary that young men who are trained at the various administrative training centres should not imbibe the feeling that they are superior to the citizenry of the country by any means. He was of the opinion that it was wrong that young probationers were made to imbibe western habits and western social standards. Encouraging young men to take to drinking, during the period of their training also was, according to him, highly undesirable. Morarji believed that if the political leadership of the country gave the right guidance and inspiration, there was not a single task that the administrators were incapable of performing efficiently. Morarji felt that politicians should not indulge in constant sniping at officials who head their departments. It was important that the ministers should ensure that efficiency was adhered to in the totality of their Ministry's functioning. Officials should be fearless in discharging their duties and should not hesitate to freely express their views in front of their superiors. Officers who are reluctant to take decisions whether out of inherent weakness or reasons of caution, he felt, must be dealt with severely; but it was equally important that officials be shielded from unmerited criticism. If that was assured, he was convinced that they would undoubtedly take quick and firm decisions.

Another facet of his administrative far-sightedness can be borne out by the fact that he made an effort to bring in professionals to posts in the government hitherto held by IAS Officers. He made an economist Manmohan Singh the Finance Secretary, a plant scientist M.S. Swaminathan the Agriculture Secretary, a chemist Lovraj Kumar, the Petroleum Secretary and an engineer Manuel Menezes the Defence Production Secretary. Unfortunately this effort of bringing outside talent into the government was given up after Morarji ceased to be Prime Minister. It was an endeavour which should have continued and been expanded upon.

On Uni-Religious Organisations or Ideologies

Morarji was quite emphatic about his views on uni-religious organisations like the RSS and Jamaat-e-Islami and felt that propagating an ideology of being limited to a Hindu Rashtra was in his view against the culture and ethos of our country. 'How would we feel if Islamic and Christian countries made us subscribe to their religions when we went there?' he asked. Journalists Kuldip Nayar and Sir Mark Tully also feel that Morarji's Gandhian beliefs and ideology would prevent him from being associated with organisations given to beliefs of the Hindu Rashtra and so on. Morarji also made a mention of the fact that during the period of the Janata Government he had tried to persuade the RSS Leaders to open their horizons and change their views on allowing other religions to join their organisation but to no avail.

His government was a government of politicians from the Socialist stream, the Lok Dal of Charan Singh, the Jan Sangh (which later became the BJP) and old Congressmen like Jagjivan Ram, H.N. Bahuguna and Biju Patnaik. It thus could not be accused of having blind commitment to any one ideology and was wedded to Gandhian Socialism.

On his Political Partners and Opponents

Morarji was not tolerant of any indiscipline in the political parties he belonged to, be it the Congress or later the Janata Party. Dr Subramaniam Swamy, who was once considered quite close to Morarji Desai, was expelled from the Janata Party in 1984 at the instance of the then Party President Chandra Shekhar. Morarji hit out at him as a politician who 'could not get even 10% votes for the election of the Presidentship of the Party.' He also took strong exception to Swamy's calling the Janata Party 'Choron ki

Party' (a party of thieves) angrily retorting, 'I am also a member of the Party.' (*Indian Express*, 12 July 1984).

Apart from Mrs Indira Gandhi (who was alive when the conversation with the author on this and other topics took place) he was critical of most opposition leaders like Chandra Shekhar, A.B. Vajpayee, and, of course, Charan Singh, who he named as the single biggest factor in bringing down his government. About Chandra Shekhar's padyatra undertaken in 1983, he believed that it was done only to project himself. He also believed that the inertia of the bureaucracy should be used positively by the political leadership without being completely dependent on them. He had repeatedly stated that as government both political and bureaucratic action must not be governed by feelings. (Later repeated in an interview to Dhiren Bhagat, published posthumously, Sunday, 23 April 1995: 'And when in government you must not become a man. You must act as the government. Otherwise you are hampered.'). He retained his wholehearted commitment to democracy and felt that dictatorship was against the natural instinct of the human being. He believed that a dictator, even if he is a saint, will become a devil as unlimited power without responsibility is bound to be unsuccessful for the wellbeing of a nation in the long run.

Sometime around 1984 a minor controversy had erupted, as Atal Bihari Vajpayee, who was then President of the BJP, had made a statement that a secret agreement had taken place when Morarji Desai had been elected leader of the Janata Parliamentary Party in 1977, where Jaya Prakash Narayan and Kripalani had decided that Morarji would be Prime Minister for half the term after which Jagjivan Ram would be Prime Minister for the rest of the government's life. When the author asked Morarji about it he called it an absolute untruth and said that he had a letter from Kripalani (about the events of March 1977) which gave no indication of this so called 'deal.' He added that Raj Narain, who proposed his name for the leadership, had told him that he had no idea about it either.

Interactions with the Press

Morarji was very particular about his monthly press conferences, unlike many of his successors who did not consider it necessary or worthy of attention, not giving these interactions the importance they deserved in a democracy. In fact apart from Jawaharlal Nehru and Morarji Desai no other Prime Minister had kept his monthly date with the media. This is a tragedy as the exchange allows the media an insight into the thoughts and viewpoints of the Prime Minister and affords the Prime Minister a view of the ground situation. What was important to Morarji was to hear the other point of view. Even his worst critics would agree that he was open to criticism and would give his opponent a fair chance to express his point of view. Some of his interactions with the media had been acerbic at times and gave evidence of his wit and humour, as also satire and irony.

A couple of instances of such question answer sessions will give the readers an insight into Morarji's style and wit:

Q: When could we expect a full Cabinet?

A: Why are you so anxious about it? None of you is a candidate.

Q: Your budget has been disappointing for the common man?

A: If there is no disappointment for you there will be no disappointment for the people.

Another comment appears to give one a different angle of his thinking. As a parting shot a pressman referred to Morarji's confessional statement that he had changed a lot after his Emergency jail term. 'What is the nature of the change?' he asked with a touch of irony. 'The change,' said Morarji, 'is that now I know you better.' Another witticism from his brushes with the Press: When asked, 'Why do you always answer a question with a question?' he promptly shot back, 'Why not?'

Morarji Desai believed in giving comprehensive statements without beating around the bush. This of course could be said for most leaders of that era. They did their homework before they spoke. The one line tweet message was something of an anathema to them. No mocking nicknames of the opponent were resorted to. Of Mrs Gandhi he once said, 'I always refer to her as Indiraben or Mrs Indira Gandhi.'

Kuldip Nayar, the eminent journalist, had some interesting anecdotes to narrate about his long association with Morarji Desai. Once Nayar, as Editor of the *Indian Express*, had written an article critical of the Janata Government. Morarji rang him up and asked him in irritation, 'Do you want Indira to come back to power?' to which Nayar retorted immediately, 'Morarjibhai if she comes back to power it will be because of the foibles of your people in government and not because of what I write.'

Nayar is reported to have said that Morarji had a knack of always answering a question with a counter question which made him a difficult person to interview. However it was also a fact that Morarji would not be found wanting in giving comprehensive answers at interviews and press conferences. Sir Mark Tully who made a film on Morarji Desai, found him quite forthcoming even on the subject of Urine Therapy. One of the persons on the Prime Minister's staff had told Tully before he started the film. 'I won't let you take the urine out of the Prime Minister,' but Morarji was more than willing to talk about the topic. He asked Tully to feel his skin which Tully found very soft. He also told him that he had written a book on Nature Cure and Urine Therapy. When Tully completed the film he showed it to Morarji at a special screening. Morarji had only one angry comment, 'Why did you give so much space to Girilal Jain?' Girilal Jain, Editor of *The Times of India* at that time, was a severe critic of the Janata Government. Tully said that he had added Jain's comments to give the film a balanced coverage so that it did not look a one-sided affair.

Summing Up

All said and done, Morarji's position will remain one of unique stature in the political history of India in the first four decades after independence. Prime Minister Nehru said of him in a letter to C.D. Deshmukh in April 1956: 'There are very few people whom I respect so much for their rectitude, ability, efficiency and fairness as Morarji Desai.'

The people of this country can no doubt, learn a lot from his exemplary life. As former Prime Minister Vishwanth Pratap Singh said, 'Morarjibhai has always held his principles very high and had never compromised them for anyone however high and mighty. He has never done anything for himself. Future generations have a lot to learn from him.'

So, how will history view Morarji Desai? On the whole it will be fairly kind to him, a few warts notwithstanding. All said and done both in the field of human endeavour and as a political leader Morarji Desai will be thought of as a Prime Minister who stuck to his principles for all times in the future. In the years to come he will be remembered more and more for his honesty and uprightness, a quality that seems to be becoming a scarce commodity.

If there ever is a poem that can aptly sum up Morarji's life it is Rudyard Kipling's 'IF'.

'If you can keep your head when all about you
Are losing theirs and blaming it on you,
If you can trust yourself when all men doubt you,
But make allowance for their doubting too;
If you can wait and not be tired by waiting,
Or being lied about, don't deal in lies,
Or being hated, don't give way to hating,
And yet don't look too good, nor talk too wise;

If you can dream and not make dreams your master,
If you can think and not make thoughts your aim;
If you can meet with Triumph and Disaster
And treat those two imposters just the same;
If you can bear to hear the truth you've spoken
Twisted by knaves to make a trap for fools,

Or watch the things you gave your life to, broken,
And stoop and build'em up with worn-out tools;

If you can make one heap of all your winnings,
And risk it on one turn of pitch-and-toss;
And lose, and start again at your beginnings
And never breathe a word about your loss;
If you can force your heart and nerve and sinew
To serve your turn long after they are gone,
And so hold on when there is nothing in you
Except the will which says to them. "Hold on."

If you can walk with crowds and keep your virtue,
Or walk with Kings-nor lose the common touch,
If neither foes nor loving friends can hurt you,
If all men count with you, but none too much;
If you can fill the unforgiving minute
With sixty second's worth of distance run,
Yours is the earth and everything that's in it
And which is more you'll be a Man, my son!

Morarji Desai as a Deputy Collector in Thane district of Bombay Presidency 1921-22. *From the autobiography of Morarji Desai*

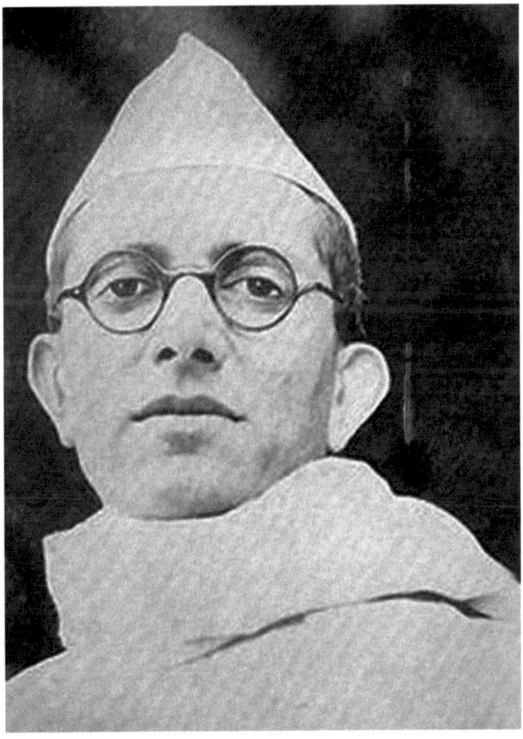

Morarji Desai as a congressman in 1937. *Courtesy: Wikipedia*

Morarji Desai as Chief Minister of Bombay State with Prime Minister Jawaharlal Nehru who is being introduced to Brigadier N. D. Bilimoria. Four Prime Ministers of India are in this picture, Jawaharlal Nehru, Indira Gandhi, Morarji Desai and Rajiv Gandhi.
Courtesy: Bilimoria Family Collection

Above: Arriving in Parliament House to present the Budget for 1962-63.
Courtesy: Photo Division, Ministry of Information & Broadcasting, Government of India.

Below: With Jawaharlal Nehru and Indira Gandhi at a dinner for Duncan Sandys, British Secretary of State for Commonwealth Relations, May 1963.
Courtesy: Photo Division, Government of India.

Above: President S. Radhakrishnan administers oath of office to Morarji Desai as Deputy Prime Minister and Minister for Finance, March 1967.
Courtesy: Photo Division, Government of India.

Below: Deputy Prime Minister Morarji Desai with Dudley Senanayake, Prime minister of Ceylon and Prime Minister Indira Gandhi at Palam Airport, November 1968.
Courtesy: Photo Division, Government of India.

Above: As Deputy Prime Minister inaugurating the All India Co-operative Week at New Delhi, November 1968. *Courtesy: Photo Division, Government of India.*

Left: The first Meter Gauge Locomotive made in India being commissioned at the Diesel Locomotive Works, Varanasi by Morarji Desai, Deputy Prime Minister, November 1968. Right, M.D. Poonacha, Union Minister for Railways. *Courtesy: Photo Division, Government of India.*

Above: Morarji Desai being sworn in as Prime Minister of India by Acting President B.D. Jatti, 24 march 1977.

Below: Inaugural Broadcast to the nation, as Prime Minister, 4 April 1977.
Courtesy: Photo Division, Government of India.

Above: Morarji Desai with Atal Bihari Vajpayee, Minister for External Affairs.
Courtesy: Photo Division, Government of India.

Below: Receiving a book from well-known journalist D.R. Mankekar, June 1977.
Courtesy: Photo Division, Government of India.

Back from the jaws of death ... arrival at Palam Airport after the air crash at Jorhat November 1977. Defence Minister Jagjivan Ram, Vice President B.D. Jatti and President N. Sanjeeva Reddy are also in the picture.
Courtesy: Photo Division, Government of India.

Above: Addressing senior Air Force Commanders, December 1977.
Courtesy: Photo Division, Government of India.

Below: Morarji Desai (third from right, front row) with US President Jimmy Carter during his January 1978 visit to India.
Courtesy: Wikipedia.

Above: Morarji Desai introducing US President Jimmy Carter to the Union Ministers, January 1978. Charan Singh, Jagjivan Ram and Biju Patnaik are in the front row. Surjit Singh Barnala can be seen in the second row.

Below: With the Shah of Iran at the Niavaran Palace, Tehran, June 1978.
Courtesy: Photo Division, Government of India.

Below: Addressing the Indian community in New York, June 1978. Minister for External Affairs, Atal Bihari Vajpayee and Indian Ambassador to the USA, Nani A. Palkhivala are also in the picture.
Courtesy: Photo Division, Government of India.

Below: With Pakistan President Zia-ul-Haq at Nairobi, August 1978.
Courtesy: Photo Division, Government of India.

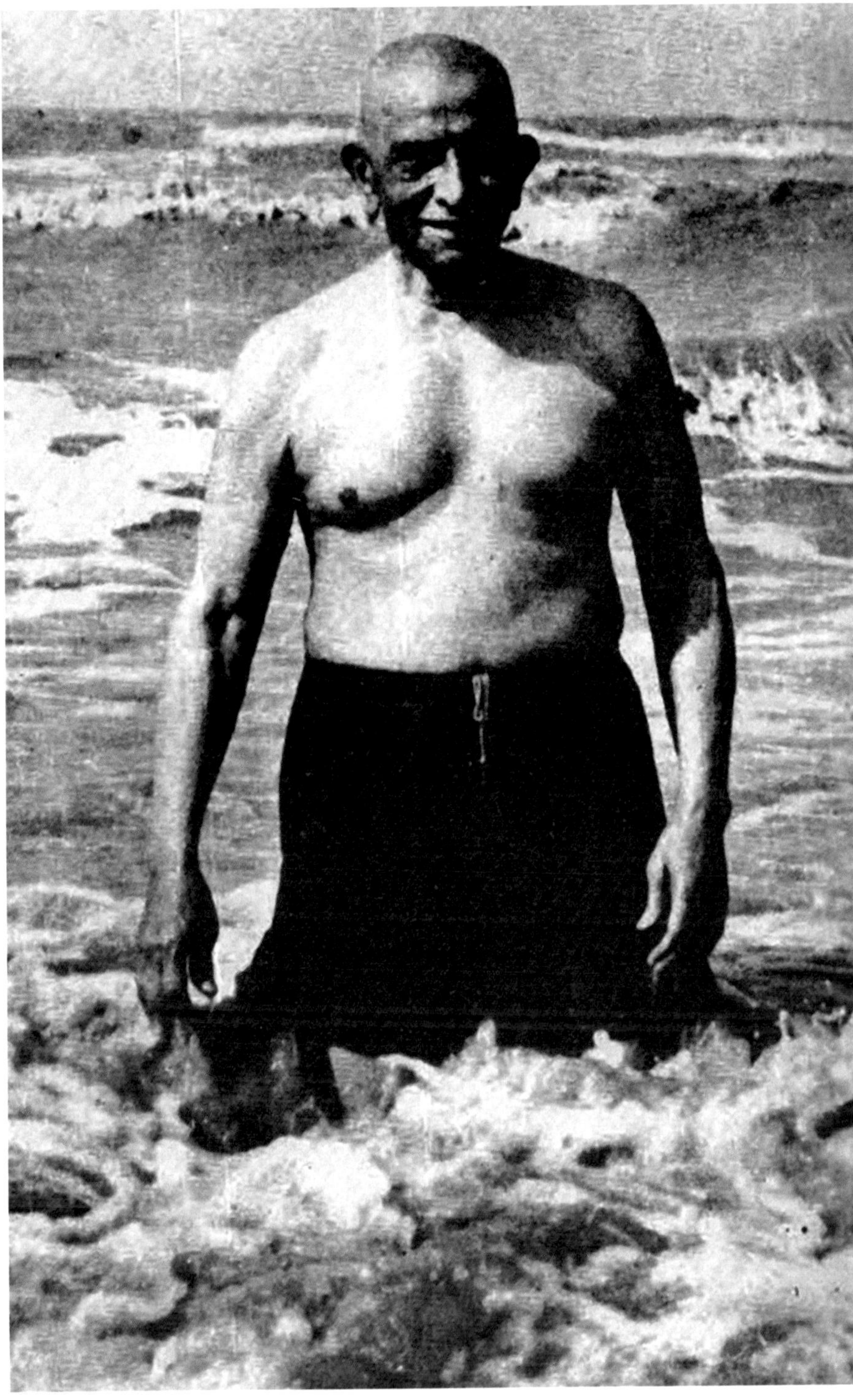

Taking a Dip in Ganga Sagar, June 1979.

Above: With the author in a jovial mood, Bombay, June 1987.
Courtesy: Author's personal collection

Below: Receiving a Tamrapatra of the Bharatiya Vidya Bhawan from President R. Venkataraman, December 1987. Also seen C. Subramaniam.
Courtesy: Photo Division, Government of India.

Above: Morarji Desai with Prime Minister V.P. Singh who called on him at his residence in Bombay, January 1990.
Courtesy: Photo Division, Government of India.

Below: With Prime Minister P.V. Narasimha Rao when the latter called to wish him on his 99th birthday, February 1995.
Courtesy: Photo Division, Government of India.

Morarji Desai's son Kantilal Desai lights the funeral pyre at Ahmedabad on 12 April 1995. His grandsons Bharat and Jagdeep also present.
Courtesy: Photo Division, Government of India.

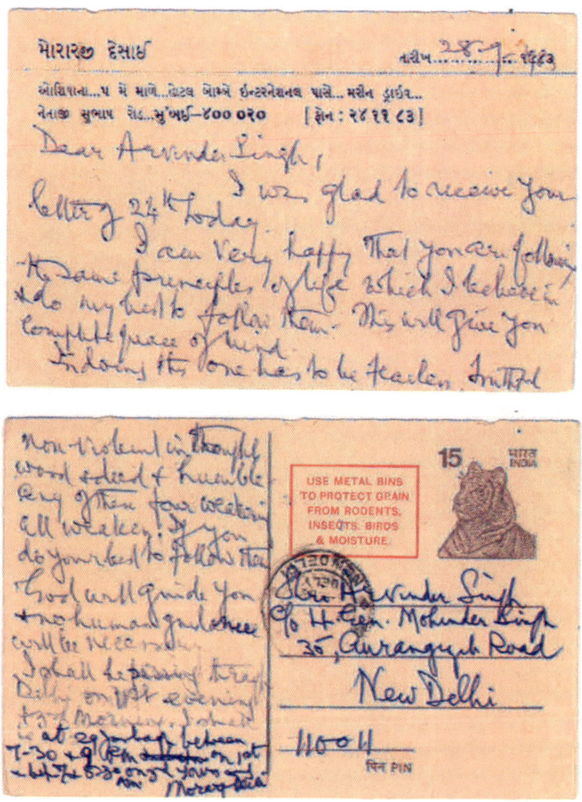

મોરારજી દેસાઈ તારીખ 28-7-૧૯૮૩

ઓશિયાના...૫ મે માળે...હોટલ ઓબેરોય ઇન્ટરનેશનલ પાસે...મરીન ડ્રાઈવ..
નેતાજી સુભાષ રોડ...મુંબઈ–૪૦૦ ૦૨૦ [ફોન : ૨૪૧૧ ૮૩]

Dear Arvinder Singh,

I was glad to receive your letter of 24th today.

I am very happy that you are following the same principles of life which I believe in & do my best to follow them. This will give you complete peace of mind.

In doing this one has to be fearless, truthful, non-violent in thought, word & deed & humble. Any of these four weakening all weaken. If you do your best to follow them God will guide you & no human guidance will be necessary.

I shall be passing through Delhi on 9th evening & 10th morning. I shall be at 29 Jorbagh between 7-30 & 9 PM on 10th [illegible]

[illegible] Yours sincerely,
Morarji Desai

Shri Arvinder Singh
C/o Lt. Gen. Mohinder Singh
35, Aurangzeb Road
New Delhi
110011
पिन PIN

Facsimile of the letter written by Morarji Desai to the author (as mentioned in the Preface).

Appendix 1

Tribute By Nani A. Palkhivala

The Sunday Observer, 16 April 1995

A Great Moral Force

The death of Morarji Desai in his hundredth year brings back to my mind the memories of this great individual, both as a man and minister: as Finance Minister and later as Prime Minister.

I have had the good fortune of coming in close contact with Morarjibhai, and also with the late Shri Jaya Prakash Narayan who was the most charismatic leader of those heady days when India was just recovering from the trauma of the Emergency.

I think, in the history of independent India, there has not been a Prime Minister who made less efforts to attain or retain that high office. The members of parliament left it to Jaya Prakashji to decide who the Prime Minister should be, and JP had no problem in choosing Morarji whom he knew to be a first class administrator, a man of total integrity and a man who had no lust for office.

During Morarji's tenure as Prime Minister, India witnessed the strange phenomenon of a fall in prices. All over the world people were wondering how India managed to bring about a drop in prices, which was described by the newspapers, in bad English, as 'negative inflation.' The then Finance Minister, the late H.M. Patel, should also be given credit along with Morarji for the recession in the cost of living.

One of Morarji's noteworthy characteristics was total frankness and fearlessness. He was not interested in the question whether others shared his views; he was strong in his convictions and true to them. He was willing, if necessary, to stand in a minority of one.

Before he became Prime Minister, Sikkim had been grabbed by the previous government and was forcibly made a part of the territory of India. The question was raised in Parliament as to whether Morarji Desai as Prime Minister of the then government thought that the action taken in Sikkim was justified and whether he agreed with it.

I remember vividly the answer which Morarjibhai gave. He was very clear. He thought the action taken in Sikkim was wholly unjustified and not worthy of a great nation like India. He rightly emphasised that it would have been better to have an agreement with the ruler of Sikkim and that it would have been a totally different matter if Sikkim had been made a part of India by persuasion and under a treaty between India and that kingdom.

There can be no doubt at all that Morarji Desai's view was the only honourable view in the matter. But though the Janata party had an overwhelming majority in Parliament, none of the members of even his own party rose to support what Morarjibhai said. Thus his voice remained the only voice of morality in international relations to be heard in parliament on that day.

Small wonder that the distinguishing feature of Morarji's tenure as prime minister was that our relations with Pakistan and Bangladesh reached the heights of friendliness and goodwill. His integrity and transparency was greatly appreciated both in Pakistan and in Bangladesh and this led to an unusual warmth of feeling between India on the one side and Pakistan and Bangladesh on the other. Sri Aurobindo's prediction that India and Pakistan are bound to come close together and share a common destiny came close to fulfilment than ever before.

Morarji never allowed the wayward barons of bureaucracy to dictate his policy either as Finance Minister or as Prime Minister. He thought it was the function of the minister to lay down the policy and it was the function of parliament to pass appropriate laws to give effect to the policy. The function of the bureaucracy was only to implement the policy.

One typical example of that was the change he made in the technique of budgeting at the Centre.

In all the previous years in our history as a Republic, the rates of tax prescribed by the Finance Bill applied to the income of the year at the end of which the Budget was introduced. Morarjibhai thought this was totally unfair and unjust to taxpayers.

He rightly took the view that the new rates prescribed by the Finance Bill should apply prospectively only to the income to be earned in the months to follow the Budget. This was against the policy dictated by the mindset of the bureaucrats up to the time when Morarjibhai changed the policy.

Since then no Finance Bill has ever attempted to go back to the old pattern. After the innovation introduced by Morarjibhai, the Finance Bill has invariably stuck to the new pattern of making the new rates of tax applicable only prospectively.

The Indian people take their moral standards from their rulers. When they had the good fortune to be governed by noble kings or leaders, they rose to lofty heights. By contrast, under corrupt kings or rulers, the Indian nation has a tendency to become correspondingly debased. This phenomenon was in evidence during the prime ministership of Morarji. History will record that he gave the necessary moral leadership and a clean administration to India. He never laid any offering on the altar of populism.

Appendix 2

Tribute By Atal Bihari Vajpayee

The Sunday Observer, 16 April 1995

The Karmayogi

Morarjibhai Desai will be remembered as the prime minister of the first non-Congress government of the country. It was he who organised the anti-Congress movement in Gujarat which resulted in the defeat of the Congress Party there and also paved the way for the defeat of the Congress in other parts of the country. So, though Jaya Prakash Narayan had played a historic role in the movement, it was Morarji who initiated the process in Gujarat.

There were three leaders in the running for prime ministership in 1977 – Morarjibhai, Jagjivan Ram and Chaudhary Charan Singh. Charan Singh wanted to be the Prime Minister, but he had come to the Centre for the first time. So his name was not seriously considered, though he himself thought he was a serious contender.

Jagjivan Ram was a strong contender; some of us favoured him because of his administrative capability and also because for the first time a member of the scheduled castes would become Prime Minister. But others did not like the idea, primarily because Jagjivan Ram was with the Congress almost till the end and had moved the resolution imposing the Emergency, in Parliament. Ultimately the matter was left to Jaya Prakash Narayan and J.B. Kripalani. Surprisingly, both were in favour of Desai. Maybe, because of his commitment to Gandhiism, maybe for other reasons.

To me, personally, that came as a surprise because I thought that Morarji was a rigid person, stubborn, not ready to compromise, and this might prove a handicap in running a coalition government composed of all sorts of elements from extreme left to extreme right.

I had never been in government before and I insisted on the External Affairs portfolio. I said either you give me External Affairs or I will not join the government because this is the only subject I am interested in, so he gave me External Affairs.

Most Prime Ministers want to be their own foreign ministers. If they are not then they guide the External Affairs ministry. But Morarjibhai seldom interfered in my ministry. He allowed all ministers a free hand. Only broad policies were decided in the Cabinet and major decisions were referred to him. But there was no interference in day-to-day functioning.

If he had a reputation for being somewhat unbending it was probably acquired when he was a civil servant. And he was certainly uncompromising on very small matters too. For instance, Charan Singh wanted to take a doctor with him while on tour. Now rules do not permit this, as wherever a minister goes in the country medical assistance is available. So Morarji did not allow the doctor to accompany Charan Singh. It was such a minor matter but it led to a tiff between the two and relations between thcm dcteriorated.

On another occasion Morarjibhai did not congratulate Charan Singh on his birthday which outraged Charan Singh. Desai's stand was that there was no point in celebrating the birthday of old people. His explanation may be satisfactory but it created a crisis in the coalition ministry!

You could say his uncompromising attitude contributed to the fall of the Janata Party government. He once received a complaint of corruption from a party member against a minister. This should have been referred to the party president Chandra Shekhar, but Morarji wanted to deal with it on the governmental level. Ultimately that minister left Morarjibhai when the split came, saying he was not given the right to reply to the allegations and the inquiry was ordered against him without taking him into confidence.

But I won't say that Morarji violated principles. In certain things he just wanted to have his own way and this came in the way of the smooth functioning of the coalition government.

There was a clash of ambitions also. Chaudhary Charan Singh wanted to become Prime Minister. Astrologers had told Morarjibhai that he would continue in office for 21 years. So even on the day when the party was to split, he was pretty confident. Not because astrologers had said so but because he believed in karma and was ready to face any situation. That way he was a marvellous man, a remarkable man who believed in karma and did not believe in *phala* (result).

No, he wasn't above ambition. He wanted to become Prime Minister and continue as Prime Minister. He often used to say there was nothing wrong in having ambition but unfair means should not be employed to achieve that ambition. He did not encourage defection. Had he made compromises, the government would not have fallen. But he stood like a rock.

He was dubbed a rightist, but Morarji was pragmatic in economic matters. He believed in the reconstruction of the economy. He was committed to swadeshi as a movement and was a staunch Gandhian, but he was not opposed to big industries as such. Though, when Coca-Cola refused to reveal their formula, he decided to oppose them. He wanted transparency.

He wasn't anti-Soviet or pro-US. I visited both countries with him and everywhere he proved himself to be an ace diplomat and succeeded in conveying that India will not compromise with its vital national interests. I remember a heated discussion with Soviet leaders. Morarji was frank enough to tell them that they should stop interfering in our internal affairs. First they lied, and later tried to defend their stand by saying that Communism being an international movement they were functioning in India also, ideologically that is.

Morarji did not accept this argument and at one stage the atmosphere became very surcharged. But in the evening, speaking at the dinner in his honour, he talked of eternal ties and friendship with the Soviet Union and all doubts were dispelled. The Soviets liked him for his frankness and straightforward dealing and for his attitude of thinking about the good of all.

As for the allegation that he was a CIA mole, Morarjibhai was a patriot of the highest order. And for $20,000? It could have been some other Desai. A clash similar to the one in Moscow had occurred in Washington too. Nani Palkhivala, our ambassador, had invited some senators and Congressmen to meet us and Morarjibhai was trying to explain to them India's economic policy. One Congressman or senator said that India could not do without US aid. Morarjibhai lost his temper and said that while India was grateful for US help it could certainly do without it. If you want to stop the aid, go ahead, he said.

I recall another incident when we were in Belgrade. Morarji was supposed to place a wreath on the monument dedicated to the Unknown Soldier which was on top of a hill. So Kantibhai asked me to place the wreath as the climb would have caused breathing problems for Morarji. I offered the wreath and as we were returning, we saw Morarjibhai toiling up the hill. He placed the wreath himself. I think that small incident gives a glimpse into his personality.

Bibliography

The Story of My Life, Morarji Desai Vol. I &II Macmillan, 1974.

The Story of My Life, Morarji Desai Vol III, S. Chand & Co. 1979.

'Morarji' by D.F. Karaka, *The Times of India*, Bombay, 1965.

In My View Morarji Desai, Thacker & Co, Bombay, 1966.

'Jack-Staying incident with Navy,' *Indian Express*, New Delhi, 31st Oct. 1977.

Jorhat Crash, *Sunday Standard*, New Delhi, 6 Nov. 1977.

USA Tour of 1978, various copies of *Indian Express/Sunday Standard* 6-18, June, 1978.

Foreign tour to U.S.S.R., Czechoslovakia, Yugoslavia and Germany, June 1979, *India Today*, 1-15 July, 1979.

Index